David N. Miller · Stephen E. Brock

Identifying, Assessing, and Treating Self-Injury at School

 Springer

David N. Miller
University at Albany
State University of New York
1400 Washington Avenue
Albany, NY 12222
USA
dmiller@uamail.albany.edu

Stephen E. Brock
Department of Special Education
Rehabilitation, School Psychology
  and Deaf Studies
California State University, Sacramento
6000 J Street
Sacramento, CA 95819-6079
USA
brock@csus.edu

ISBN 978-1-4419-6091-7 (hardcover)   e-ISBN 978-1-4419-6092-4
ISBN 978-1-4419-9512-4 (softcover)
DOI 10.1007/978-1-4419-6092-4
Springer New York Dordrecht Heidelberg London

Library of Congress Control Number: 2010929849

Springer is part of Springer Science+Business Media (www.springer.com)

Developmental Psychopathology at School

Series Editors

Stephen E. Brock
California State University, Sacramento, CA, USA

Shane R. Jimerson
University of California, Santa Barbara, CA, USA

For further volumes:
http://www.springer.com/series/7495

With love and gratitude to my wife Kris; to the memory of my mother, Mary J. Miller; and in honor of my father, Donald A. Miller (D.N.M.).

To the memory of Christine Jane Bibbes Brock (S.E.B.).

And to all students and their families challenged by self-injury and the school-based professionals committed to helping them.

Acknowledgments

As authors of this book, we would like to acknowledge and thank the many individuals who contributed to our efforts and made our work much easier in the process. First and foremost, David Miller would like to thank his spouse, Kristin Miller of Siena College, for providing helpful suggestions throughout the writing of this book. Without her constant encouragement and unwavering support, this book would not have been written. He would also like to acknowledge his friend and colleague Richard Lieberman, school psychologist and coordinator of the Suicide Prevention Unit of the Los Angeles Unified School District, for his school-based writings on self-injury and his contributions to Chapter 2 of this book; Ryan R. Lindsay, Clinical Director of the St. Louis Center for Family Development, for his recommendations regarding useful Web sites on self-injury; and Nancy L. Heath, Mary K. Nixon, and Barent W. Walsh, all nationally recognized authorities on self-injury, whose publications on this topic significantly influenced the contents of this book. In addition, he would like to thank Donald A. Miller for a timely newspaper article; Brad Arndt for his information on Lesch–Nyhan Disease; the students, faculty, and staff at Centennial School of Lehigh University, particularly Michael George, for providing him with excellent training opportunities; and University at Albany, SUNY school psychology graduate students Kristin Darius-Anderson, Jeannette Ellis, Cara Pharr-Gottheim, Erin Pinto, Jaime Savoie, and Kevin White for their assistance. Finally, he would like to acknowledge Stephen Brock and Shane Jimerson, editors of the Developmental Psychopathology at School Series, for their interest in adding a book on self-injury to this distinguished series. Stephen Brock deserves special thanks for his support of this book and his willingness to serve as second author on it.

Stephen Brock would also like to thank his good friend and colleague Richard Lieberman as well as Linda Kanan, Jennifer Finger, and Amy Plog of the Cherry Creek School District in Colorado, for their groundbreaking work applying self-injury scholarship to the school setting. In addition, he would like to acknowledge the superior scholarship of lead author David Miller and the editorial support of Dr. Shane Jimerson. Dr. Brock would also like to thank Drs. Miller and Jimerson for their understanding and patience during what was a very difficult final year of this book's preparation. It was an honor and a pleasure working with them on this project.

Finally, both Drs. Miller and Brock would like to acknowledge the many researchers and practitioners who provided the foundation for the material presented in this book.

Contents

About the Author

Stephen E. Brock, Ph.D., NCSP, is an associate professor at California State University, Sacramento. Previously, he worked for 18 years as a school psychologist with the Lodi Unified School District (the last six of which included assignments as lead psychologist). His professional preparation includes a Ph.D. at the University of California, Davis. Dr. Brock currently serves on the editorial boards of both state and national school psychology association newsletters and was an associate editor of The California School Psychologist (a peer-reviewed journal with the second largest distribution of school psychology journals in the United States). He is past-president of the California Association of School Psychologists and was member of the National Association of School Psychologists' Delegate Assembly and its Executive Council. Dr. Brock has authored more than 150 publications (including nine books) and has made more than 100 refereed or invited state/national conference presentations. His academic work has included the study of school crisis response, suicide prevention, ADHD, autism, behavioral interventions, violence prevention, threat assessment, child development, and reading comprehension.

David N. Miller, Ph.D, is an assistant professor in the Department of Educational and Counseling Psychology at the University at Albany, State University of New York. He received his Ph.D. in school psychology from Lehigh University. A certified school psychologist, he has extensive experience working with students with emotional and behavioral problems in both public and alternative school settings, including serving as the director of the Predoctoral Internship in Professional Psychology at Centennial School of Lehigh University. He has more than 30 professional publications and book chapters and has conducted more than 40 national and state presentations on various topics, including self-injury and suicidal behavior in children and youth. He was also co-chair of the Suicide Prevention/Intervention Workgroup of the National Association of School Psychologists School Crisis Prevention and Intervention Task Force. Dr. Miller currently serves on the editorial advisory board of School Psychology Review, Psychology in the Schools, School Psychology Forum, and the Division 16 (School Psychology) Book Series.

Chapter 1
Introduction

Self-injury refers to the intentional, purposeful, and socially unacceptable infliction of bodily harm without suicidal intent (Klonsky, 2007; Nixon & Heath, 2009a; Walsh, 2006). Also known as non-suicidal self-injury (NSSI; Nock, 2009), it is a puzzling, disturbing, and often poorly understood behavior prevalent in all cultures and across all socioeconomic levels (Lieberman & Poland, 2006). Although the first recorded account of NSSI occurred over 2,400 years ago (Favazza, 1998), it has only been in recent decades that this condition has received widespread attention from professionals and the general public. The most common form of NSSI appears to be skin cutting (Klonsky & Muehlenkamp, 2007), and most individuals who engage in it typically cut on their forearms, although it is not necessarily restricted to that area (Nixon & Heath, 2009a). NSSI may take other forms as well, including severe skin scratching, picking at wounds, inserting objects into the body, or banging one's head (D'Onofrio, 2007). This last behavior, however, is more typically observed among students with severe developmental disabilities (Brock, Jimerson, & Hansen, 2006) and is different from the type of NSSI examined in this book.

NSSI has been referred to by a variety of descriptors, including self-mutilation, deliberate self-harm, non-suicidal self-harm, parasuicide, self-wounding, wrist-cutter syndrome, self-carving, self-cutting, repetitive non-suicidal self-injurious behavior, self-inflicted violence, and self-abuse (Favazza, 1996; Nixon & Heath, 2009a; Walsh, 2006). Additionally, because the most prominent method of body tissue self-destruction among individuals who engage in NSSI appears to be skin cutting with a knife or other sharp objects, these students often are colloquially referred to as "cutters" (Lieberman, 2004). The term *self-injury* is currently the most widely used and accepted designation for these behaviors (D'Onofrio, 2007; Nixon & Heath, 2009b; Walsh, 2006) and is the one that is used in this book. Both individuals who engage in NSSI and those who treat them have advocated that the term "self-mutilation" – previously the most common descriptor – be discontinued because it typically is too extreme, pejorative, and ultimately inaccurate (Simeon & Favazza, 2001; Walsh, 2006).

Although it may occur at any age, NSSI is associated with adolescence because it typically emerges during this developmental period (Nixon & Heath, 2009a). As a result, it has become a major concern among adults who work with children and youth, particularly school-based professionals. In fact, schools have emerged as the

D.N. Miller, S.E. Brock, *Identifying, Assessing, and Treating Self-Injury at School*,
Developmental Psychopathology at School, DOI 10.1007/978-1-4419-6092-4_1,
© Springer Science+Business Media, LLC 2010

primary place in which children and adolescents who engage in NSSI first come to the attention of others and therefore is the setting in which an effective response often begins (D'Onofrio, 2007; Lieberman, Toste, & Heath, 2009). Consequently, it is likely that schools will be increasingly asked to take a more active role in the identification, assessment, and treatment of students with NSSI.

There has been a tremendous increase in the amount of attention given to NSSI in recent years, including the publication of several books (e.g., Bowman & Randall, 2006; Conterio & Lader, 1998; D'Onofrio, 2007; Levenkron, 1998; Nixon & Heath, 2009b; Nock, 2009; Plante, 2007; Simeon & Hollander, 2001; Strong, 1998; Walsh, 2006), self-help guides (e.g., Alderman, 1997; Clarke, 1999; Shapiro, 2008; Winkler, 2003), memoirs (e.g., Carney, 2005; Kettlewell, 1999; Vega, 2007), young adult novels (e.g., Carlson, 2005; McCormick, 2000), parent guides (e.g., Hollander, 2008; McVey-Noble, 2006), and newspaper articles (e.g., Wilber, 2007). The number of articles and book chapters directed toward school-based practitioners has increased as well (e.g., Kanan, Finger, & Plog, 2008; Lieberman, 2004; Lieberman & Poland, 2006; Lieberman et al., 2009; Miller & McConaughy, 2005; Shapiro, 2008), although as far as the authors are aware this is the first book specifically and exclusively addressed to school-based practice and NSSI.

If not effectively treated, NSSI can persist for years and even decades, and its presence increases risk for a variety of mental health and school adjustment problems (D'Onofrio, 2007). Consequently, school-based mental health professionals are being increasingly called upon to assess and respond to students engaging in NSSI, as well as to consult with teachers, other school practitioners, and parents/caregivers (Lieberman et al., 2009; Lieberman & Poland, 2006). However, because of a lack of adequate training, school-based professionals may be ill-prepared to effectively respond to NSSI (Heath, Toste, & Beetham, 2006; Miller & Jome, 2008, in press).

This situation is made more difficult by the most typical forms of NSSI (i.e., cutting, burning), which are often perceived by school personnel as shocking, repulsive, perplexing, and/or inexplicable (Walsh, 2006). Students who engage in NSSI frequently evoke powerful reactions among adults, including fear, confusion, and anger, and as a result it often distracts and distances professionals from being present and responsive to students in need of help (D'Onofrio, 2007; Walsh, 2006). Further complicating these matters is the finding that NSSI can appear contagious, potentially running through schools, peer groups, and/or grade levels (Lieberman & Poland, 2006). Consequently, it is essential that school professionals become more knowledgeable about this condition, and particularly how it is effectively assessed, identified, and treated.

Why School Professionals Should Read This Book

First, students engaging in NSSI are increasingly coming to the attention of school personnel, and as noted previously many of them report being ill-equipped to respond due to inadequate knowledge or training in this area (Heath et al., 2006;

Miller & Jome, 2008, in press). Second, to appropriately address the needs of *all* school-age youth, school psychologists and other school professionals need to be adequately prepared to identify, assess, and treat NSSI in the school setting. This section reviews some of the key issues regarding the importance of addressing the needs of these students.

Ethical and legal obligations. School personnel have an ethical and legal duty to protect students from reasonably foreseeable risk of harm, including self-harm (Jacob, 2009; Jacob & Hartshorne, 2007). Although the assessment of whether a student poses a danger to self is not always an easy task, school professionals are ethically obligated to do as much as possible to ensure that students in schools are safe from harm, including students who engage in NSSI.

Self-injury is associated with mental health and school adjustment problems. NSSI is associated with a number of other mental health problems that may negatively impact school adjustment, including suicidal behavior, mood and anxiety disorders, eating disorders, and anger and hostility (D'Onofrio, 2007; Lofthouse, Muehlenkamp, & Adler, 2009; Walsh, 2006). Like these other associated conditions, NSSI can also have a detrimental effect on educational areas such as school attendance, grades, and school completion.

Students who engage in NSSI are found in both general and special education classrooms. Typically, students with NSSI are placed in general education classrooms. However, given that these students are at risk for a host of other educational, emotional, and behavioral problems, some students with NSSI receive special education services. Consequently, school professionals serving both general and special education students need to be cognizant of information regarding NSSI and how it is effectively identified, assessed, and treated.

School professionals have daily opportunities to support students with NSSI. Many youth who engage in NSSI do not receive adequate mental health services in their communities, and many others will not even attempt to access these services because they may not view themselves as needing assistance or because they are attempting to conceal their condition. As a result, schools should, and likely will, be given a greater responsibility to identify, assess, and even treat students with NSSI. Given that most children and youth with NSSI attend school, there are daily opportunities to establish school-based support services to help address the needs of these students. School professionals thus have a unique opportunity to help facilitate more adaptive behaviors among children and youth engaging in NSSI.

Effective identification and treatment is critical. Youth who are not effectively treated for their mental health problems, including NSSI, frequently generate long-term economic costs. For example, costs associated with untreated trauma-related alcohol and drug abuse alone is estimated at over 160 billion dollars annually (Harwood, 2000). Although the long-term costs of not treating NSSI have not been quantified, given what we know about other untreated mental health challenges such as substance abuse, this amount is undoubtedly substantial. Responding early and effectively to NSSI would likely reduce its long-term economic costs. In addition, failure to effectively identify and treat NSSI may lead to negative or even tragic outcomes that extend well beyond economics. For example, engaging in repeated

NSSI clearly increases the risk for later suicidal behavior (Joiner, 2005; Joiner, Van Orden, Witte, & Rudd, 2009).

Previous books on self-injury have not focused on school-based practitioners. Although many texts on NSSI have recently been published, most of them have been directed to a wide variety of professionals, including clinical and counseling psychologists, social workers, college and university counselors, nurses, and other mental health and medical practitioners (e.g., D'Onofrio, 2007; Nixon & Heath, 2009b; Walsh, 2006). Fewer texts have specifically addressed school personnel, and none to date have focused exclusively on this population. Thus, this book is designed specifically for school practitioners and is the first to address the identification, assessment, and treatment of NSSI completely from a school-based perspective.

Self-Injury Defined

Although a brief definition of NSSI was provided at the beginning of this chapter, it is important to provide a more precise and comprehensive definition, clearly delineating what this term includes as well as what it does not. Adequately defining NSSI is more difficult than it may initially appear. It is critical, however, that school professionals have a clear understanding of the emotional and behavioral characteristics of NSSI so an effective response may be provided. The lack of standardized definitions in the past has led to a number of problems, including those potentially affecting the accuracy of reported prevalence rates, the understanding of specific correlates and predictors, and the effective planning and evaluation of interventions (Nixon & Heath, 2009a).

First and foremost, unlike many other emotional and behavioral disorders exhibited by children and adolescents (e.g., attention-deficit/hyperactivity disorder, conduct disorder, posttraumatic stress disorder), NSSI is not currently listed as a separate disorder in the *Diagnostic and Statistical Manual of Mental Disorders* (Text Rev., 4th ed.; DSM IV-TR; American Psychiatric Association [APA], 2000). Although there are plans to include NSSI as a separate and distinct disorder in the next (fifth) version of the DSM, this version is not scheduled for publication until 2013. Infact, until recently NSSI has rarely been examined as a phenomenon in itself, but rather was associated with other forms of psychopathology, particularly borderline personality disorder, suicidality, and depression (D'Onofrio, 2007; Favazza, 1998). NSSI has also frequently been associated with trauma and child maltreatment, particularly sexual abuse, although the relationship between these two conditions is not as strong as previously believed (Klonsky & Moyer, 2008). Providing a formal definition of NSSI therefore presents some unique and interesting challenges.

In this book we employ Walsh's (2006) definition, which states that NSSI is an "intentional, self-effected, low-lethality bodily harm of a socially unacceptable nature, performed to reduce psychological distress" (p. 4). This definition requires some additional explanation to ensure adequate understanding. First, critical to this definition is the word "intentional," which indicates that NSSI is deliberate rather than accidental or ambiguous in intent. Second, NSSI is suggested to be "self-effected." This term is used rather than "self-inflicted" because many individuals who engage in NSSI do so with the assistance of others. Third, the use of the phrase "low-lethality" is important, as it makes clear that NSSI is not a suicidal behavior. Fourth, NSSI is primarily about "bodily harm." An individual may talk about, plan, or attempt to self-injure, but until a student actually engages in bodily self-injury there is no NSSI.

Fifth, the phrase "of a socially unacceptable nature" emphasizes social context. In most cultures, body modification (e.g., body piercings, tattoos) is a symbolically meaningful, culturally endorsed activity. It may also have profound religious significance for some individuals, and may even serve as a rite of passage (Favazza, 1996; Walsh, 2006). This is not the case with NSSI; although it may have many meanings for the individuals who engage in it, self-injury is not endorsed by the prevailing dominant culture. Additionally, although there may be considerable social reinforcement among some groups of students for engaging in NSSI, there are no organized, culturally sanctioned rituals that surround it, and NSSI is not connected to any socially endorsed rites of passage within the culture at large (Walsh, 2006).

Finally, Walsh's definition indicates that this behavior is performed "to reduce psychological stress." Thus, understanding NSSI requires that attention be given to contextual features and its functions as well as its forms (Klonsky, 2007; Nock & Prinstein, 2005). Walsh and others (e.g., Favazza, 1996, 1998; Lieberman, 2004; Lieberman & Poland, 2006) have described how NSSI is typically enacted in an attempt to modify and ultimately reduce psychological pain and discomfort. After engaging in NSSI, individuals often report this behavior to be immediately and significantly effective in reducing pain; the behavior is reinforced and therefore often repeated. As such, the behavior is not suicidal in intent, but it is psychologically motivated, and it cannot be explained by biological mechanisms alone. Rather, it is a "self-conscious, self-intentioned, distress-reduction behavior" (Walsh, 2006, p. 5). NSSI can also serve other psychological functions, including that of gaining attention from others in the individual's environment (Jacobson & Gould, 2007), although this should be understood in its appropriate context. A common myth about NSSI is that adolescents engage in it *primarily* or even *exclusively* for attention or to manipulate others, which is clearly an overgeneralization (Froeschle & Moyer, 2004). In fact, many if not most individuals who engage in NSSI, particularly those in clinical samples, actively attempt to conceal their behavior from others. Finally, in many cases NSSI may serve multiple psychological functions (e.g., primarily distress reduction and secondarily attention).

From this definition, NSSI can be conceptualized as an internalizing (rather than an externalizing) behavior problem, given that (a) it is largely developed and maintained within an individual, and (b) it is characterized by overcontrolled symptoms (i.e., when individuals attempt to maintain too much or inappropriate control or regulation of their internal emotional and cognitive states), typically covert behavior, and a high degree of subjective distress (Merrell, 2008a). The emotional and psychological pain of the individual engaging in NSSI is often highly intense and uncomfortable, but it generally does not reach the level of a suicidal crisis (Walsh, 2006). Unlike a suicidal individual, who often experiences psychological pain as permanent and unalterable, the self-injurer typically experiences such pain as interruptible and intermittent (Walsh, 2006). However, this does not mean that NSSI and suicidal behavior are mutually exclusive. Indeed, engaging in NSSI clearly places an individual at increased risk for suicidal behavior (Joiner, 2005; Joiner et al., 2009), particularly suicide attempts (Jacobson & Gould, 2007). Nevertheless, these two forms of deliberate self-harm (i.e., NSSI and suicidal behavior) typically serve different functions.

It is also useful to understand common misconceptions about self-injury. For example, in addition to sometimes confusing it with suicidal behavior and assuming that its primary purpose is to gain attention or manipulate others, many mental health professionals mistakenly view NSSI as synonymous with borderline personality disorder, a condition that is diagnosed more often in girls and women than boys and men, and is characterized by significant fears of abandonment (APA, 2000). Although individuals with borderline personality disorder often exhibit NSSI, this diagnosis is not appropriate for the majority of youth who engage in it (Walsh, 2006). Similarly, NSSI should not be confused with what is commonly referred to as self-injurious behavior (SIB), which often is associated with children and youth with severe developmental disabilities (Brock, Jimerson et al., 2006).

Consequently, for the purposes of this book, NSSI is discussed only in the context of noncognitively impaired youth. NSSI also should be distinguished from Lesch–Nyhan Disease (Lesch & Nyhan, 1964), a rare genetic disorder resulting in a number of involuntary muscle movements, cerebral palsy, and the frequent self-mutilation of body tissue (Little & Rodemaker, 1998). Moreover, NSSI as defined in this text should not be confused with a recently recognized condition known as Body Integrity Identity Disorder (Johnson, Brett, Roberts, & Wassersug, 2007), which is characterized by the strong desire to amputate healthy limbs. Finally, NSSI should be distinguished from the culturally sanctioned forms of body modification previously described, such as body piercings or tattoos.

Self-Injury, Special Education Eligibility, and Educational Support Services

As noted above, NSSI currently is not listed as a separate diagnostic category in the *DSM IV-TR* (APA, 2000). Even if it were, it is important to realize that *DSM* diagnoses are not synonymous with special education eligibility (Fogt, Miller, & Zirkel, 2003; House, 1999, 2002). Similarly, NSSI is not listed as one of the 13 categories of disability eligible for special education services as outlined by the *Individuals with Disabilities Education Improvement Act* (IDEIA, 2004). Further, many students who engage in NSSI may not exhibit particular academic or behavioral problems that would lead to their referral to or placement in special education (Walsh, 2006).

However, this does not mean that students with NSSI would not or should not qualify for special education services. They may qualify, but only if they meet eligibility criteria for a particular handicapping condition within *IDEIA*, such as Emotionally Disturbed (ED), or Other Health Impaired (OHI). At the present time, the degree to which students with NSSI are placed in special education programs, and the educational classification(s) they most commonly receive is not clear.

School-based professionals should be cognizant of several caveats in considering special education services for students with NSSI. First, *IDEIA* requirements stipulate that a particular condition must adversely affect a child's educational performance before a student is eligible to receive special education services. NSSI may be centrally related, peripherally related, or completely unrelated to a student's level of academic achievement in school. For example, a student could be regularly engaging in NSSI yet still achieve at appropriate academic levels, thus contraindicating the provision of special education services. Conversely, a student may be engaging in NSSI to a degree that is significantly impairing his or her educational performance, and as a result special education services may be recommended.

Second, given the frequently poor outcomes associated with students placed in special education classrooms (Kavale & Forness, 1999), professionals should carefully consider whether placement in special education is necessary and appropriate for students with NSSI. In particular, school psychologists and other school-based professionals should be aware that effective special education support services are less about the "place" in which instruction occurs and more about the quality of instruction and support provided (Schulte, Osborne, & Erchul, 1998). Outcomes for students with mild disabilities (e.g., learning disabilities; emotional disturbance) placed in special education are generally poor (Kavale & Forness, 1999; Schulte et al., 1998), and there is no reason to suspect these outcomes would be any different for students with NSSI. Third, placement in special education may be stigmatizing for some students, potentially contributing to an increase in negative academic and behavioral outcomes (Jacob & Hartshorne, 2007).

As with any student for whom special education is being considered, students with NSSI should be carefully evaluated by a school psychologist as well as other professionals. If it is determined that a student with NSSI requires special education services, an educational plan based on individualized need should be collaboratively developed among school professionals, the student, and his or her parents/caregivers. Any Individualized Educational Plans (IEPs) that are developed for students with NSSI should contain treatment goals that are observable, measurable, and quantifiable. Further, only academic and behavioral interventions that are socially valid and evidence-based (i.e., those that have some degree of empirical support in the professional literature for their effectiveness) should be considered, recommended, and implemented, and these interventions should be regularly monitored, evaluated, and modified as needed.

Finally, school professionals should realize that students with NSSI may be eligible for educational accommodations under Section 504 of the Rehabilitation Act of 1973. In contrast to *IDEIA* eligibility, under 504 a *handicapped person* is defined as any individual who has a physical or mental impairment that substantially limits one or more of his or her major life activities. Hence, *handicapped* under section 504 is defined more broadly than *disability* under *IDEIA* (Jacob & Hartshorne, 2007). Students with NSSI may qualify for 504 services under the *mental impairment* criteria, which would include any mental or psychological disorder, such as a particular mental health problem or a specific learning disability (Jacob & Hartshorne, 2007). This would allow students with NSSI to receive instructional accommodations or other services designed to better meet their individual needs.

Purpose and Plan of This Book

This book is designed to provide school-based professionals with the information they need to be better prepared to identify, assess, and treat students with NSSI. Chapter 2 provides an overview of the complex and multifaceted causes of NSSI, with particular emphasis given to environmental, functional, and biopsychosocial models. Chapter 3 provides information regarding the prevalence of NSSI as well as a review of common associated conditions. Chapter 4 provides information about early screening for NSSI as well as possible risk factors and warning signs. Chapters 5 and 6 discuss assessment issues related to NSSI, including a review of various methods for assisting in diagnostic decision making and linking assessment to intervention. Finally, Chapter 7 provides a summary of how school personnel can most effectively respond to students engaging in NSSI, as well as research examining the effectiveness of interventions for this problem, with a particular emphasis on the possible roles of school-based professionals in this process.

Chapter 2
Causes *(with Richard Lieberman)*

There is no single cause of NSSI in youth that reliably determines whether a child or adolescent will ultimately engage in these behaviors. Psychiatric problems and disorders often result from complex interactions of genetic predispositions, environmental events/stressors, and individual vulnerabilities, and the causes of NSSI are no different. This chapter begins with a review of several explanatory models for NSSI in youth, with a particular emphasis on the environmental/functional model, as this approach has the most support in the professional literature. Following this discussion, a comprehensive biopsychosocial framework developed by Walsh (2006) for understanding the causal variables contributing to the development of NSSI will be described. This framework leads directly to many of the recommended assessment and treatment techniques described in subsequent chapters.

Explanatory Models for NSSI in Youth

A number of explanatory models for NSSI have been offered, and below we briefly summarize seven that have appeared most frequently in the professional literature. The models are presented in order from those with the most empirical support to those with the least, based on a recent and comprehensive critical review of the literature from 1980 through 2007 (Messer & Fremouw, 2008).

The Behavioral/Environmental Model

This model focuses on environmental contingencies that both initiate and maintain NSSI behavior (Messer & Fremouw, 2008). According to this model, NSSI occurs as a result of negative reinforcement (i.e., escaping from unpleasant or distressful feelings) or positive reinforcement (e.g., obtaining attention). This model is closely aligned with the affect regulation model and has received increasing support within the empirical literature (Messer & Fremouw, 2008). In particular, there is increasing

D.N. Miller, S.E. Brock, *Identifying, Assessing, and Treating Self-Injury at School*, Developmental Psychopathology at School, DOI 10.1007/978-1-4419-6092-4_2, © Springer Science+Business Media, LLC 2010

evidence that a functional approach to understanding and assessing NSSI is beneficial (Nock & Prinstein, 2004, 2005) and that this environmental model is useful
for linking assessment to intervention. Given that this model currently has the most
empirical support in the professional literature, in the next section we provide a more
detailed description of it. Additional information regarding a functional approach to
the assessment of NSSI is provided in Chapter 6.

The Affect Regulation Model

Several emotional states have been found to precede NSSI, including increased tension and anxiety, hostility, and feelings of depersonalization (Messer & Fremouw,
2008). Suyemoto (1998) used the term "affect regulation" in the context of NSSI
to include the regulation of pain as well as anxiety and hostility. Others have used
the terms "emotional regulation" or "mood regulation" in describing this model
(Messer & Fremouw, 2008), although to date no general consensus regarding the
accepted terminology for it has been proposed (Klonsky, 2007). There is increasing support for this model in the professional literature (Messer & Fremouw, 2008;
Walsh, 2006). It also appears to be strongly related to the behavioral/environmental
model.

The Physiological/Biological Model

The majority of explanatory models of NSSI emphasize the critical role of psychological factors, although recent evidence has suggested that biological factors may
contribute as well (Messer & Fremouw, 2008). In particular, it has been posited that
there is a biological vulnerability for engaging in NSSI either due to a dysfunctional
neurotransmitter system or an abnormal psychophysiological response to NSSI that
involves the reduction of tension (Haines, Williams, Brain, & Wilson, 1995; Stanley,
Winchel, Molcho, Simeon, & Stanley, 1992; Winchel & Stanley, 1991). As such,
there appears to be increasing evidence that biological vulnerabilities may increase
the likelihood of youth engaging in NSSI (Messer & Fremouw, 2008). This issue
is discussed in greater detail within the context of Walsh's (2006) model of NSSI
presented later in this chapter.

The Suicide Model

The suicide model posits that SI acts are actually attempts to forego or avoid suicide,
and views NSSI and suicidal behavior to be on a continuum (Messer & Fremouw,
2008). For example, Firestone and Seiden (1990) present a continuum of negative thought patterns and behaviors that ultimately culminate in suicidal plans and
attempts. It is possible that self-injury would be included in this model, although
Fireston and Seiden do not explicitly mention self-injury. Research indicates that the

relationship between youth suicidal behavior and NSSI is a complex one (Jacobson & Gould, 2007). This relationship is discussed more extensively in the next chapter.

The Interpersonal/Systemic Model

This model emphasizes NSSI as being symptomatic of family or environmental dysfunction (Messer & Fremouw, 2008). For example, an adolescent is believed to engage in NSSI in an attempt to cope with this dysfunction, or possibly to gain attention from others in the individual's environment. The "system" involved may be the family, although it could be another system, such as a residential treatment facility or a hospital environment. Further, the environment may be unknowingly supporting or reinforcing NSSI behavior (Suyemoto & MacDonald, 1995). Given that there are only a few non-experimental case studies in this area (i.e., Crouch & Wright, 2004; Hartman, 1996), conclusions regarding the viability of the interpersonal/systemic model of NSSI cannot be made at this time (Messer & Fremouw, 2008).

The Depersonalization Model

This model focuses on the psychological state of dissociation or depersonalization reportedly experienced by youth who engage in NSSI (Suyemoto & MacDonald, 1995). In particular, feelings of dissociation are assumed to result from feelings of abandonment or isolation, which in turn leads to feelings of unreality or numbness. As a result, it is assumed that youth engage in NSSI to end the experience of depersonalization and regain a sense of self (Messer & Frenmouw, 2008). From this theoretical perspective, it has been suggested that the scars that may result from engaging in NSSI may serve as reminders to the individual of their identity (Miller & Bashkin, 1974). Although a possible linkage between dissociation and NSSI is frequently referred to in the literature (e.g., D'Onofrio, 2007), there is little empirical support for this relationship, an issue that is discussed more extensively in Chapter 3.

The Sexual/Sadomasochism Model

This model emphasizes the importance of sexual development and sexuality concerns as primary causal mechanisms for NSSI. In this model, NSSI behavior is viewed as a means of providing sexual gratification, or as an attempt to control sexual development or punish sexual feelings (Messer & Fremouw, 2008). Additionally, NSSI within this model is associated with issues related to sexual confusion and body image (Zila & Kiselica, 2001). There is little or no empirical support for this model; much of the support that does exist stems from flawed case studies and studies with small numbers of hospitalized females (Messer & Fremouw, 2008).

A Functional Model of NSSI

Several important factors must be considered in discussing a functional model of NSSI. First, NSSI must be viewed within its context, in the sense that an individual is inextricably tied to his or her environment (Lloyd-Richardson, Nock, & Prinstein, 2009). To understand NSSI, it is necessary to understand why a particular behavior, at a particular time, serves a particular function for a particular individual (Suyemoto, 1998). Consequently, the reasons an individual may engage in self-injury (i.e., the function it serves) may vary over time and context. It is likely that changes may take place in youth as they experiment with self-injury, altering the functions served by it (Lloyd-Richardson et al., 2009).

Second, NSSI may serve multiple functions simultaneously (Lloyd-Richardson et al., 2009). For example, in a study evaluating motivations for both suicide attempts and NSSI in a sample of 75 women diagnosed with Borderline Personality Disorder, overall reasons for NSSI differed from those for suicide attempts, with the former endorsing an average of 10 reasons for their latest NSSI episode, most frequently described as (a) intending to express anger; (b) punishing oneself; (c) generating normal feelings; and (d) distracting oneself (Brown, Comtois, & Linehan, 2002). Although recent literature reviews provide empirical support for various functions of NSSI, the relationships (both theoretical and empirical) between these various functions remains unclear (Klonsky, 2007). Unfortunately, it can be a very challenging task to tease apart the specific and various functions NSSI may serve for an individual. However, our understanding of these possible functions is critical for altering future behaviors and improving the lives of those youth engaging in NSSI (Lloyd-Richardson et al., 2009).

A third issue involves the current lack of understanding regarding NSSI among youth. In particular, it is not clear how functional models of NSSI may be relevant to various youth populations, and to what degree, if any, they may deviate from functional models based on adult samples (Lloyd-Richardson et al., 2009). Finally, Lloyd-Richardson and colleagues (2009) mention two other factors that have limited research on the functions of NSSI. First, many authors have used the term *function* in different ways, an issue that can lead to confusion among researchers and clinicians and in explaining NSSI to individuals exhibiting it as well as to the general public. From the perspective of behavioral psychology and therapy, "function" refers to an analysis of the effects or events that cause or determine a particular behavior (Lloyd-Richardson et al., 2009). The goal of the practitioner is to examine the *antecedents* and *consequences* of a behavior to understand and treat it. It is from this behavioral (operant) tradition (Skinner, 1938, 1953) that *functional analyses* or *behavioral analyses* were derived. Much of the earlier work on

NSSI used the term *functional* more loosely, often to simply mean the purpose of or reason for a particular behavior. For example, the suggestion that NSSI serves an "anti-suicide" function says little about the antecedents or consequences of NSSI (Lloyd-Richardson et al., 2009). A second limitation is that although multiple functions of NSSI have been proposed, there have been few attempts to integrate these into a coherent theoretical model that can inform both research and practice (Lloyd-Richardson et al., 2009).

To address the issues and limitations noted above, Lloyd-Richardson and colleagues (2009) recently developed a comprehensive, four-function model of NSSI among adolescents that draws from previous work on learning theory and behavior therapy (Nock & Prinstein, 2004, 2005), as well as research on the functions of NSSI among samples of individuals with developmental disabilities (Iwata et al., 1994) and adult women diagnosed with borderline personality disorder (Brown et al., 2002). In their model, the functions of NSSI are proposed to differ along two dichotomous dimensions: (a) negative reinforcement or positive reinforcement; and (b) consequences that are either automatic (i.e., intrapersonal) or social (i.e., interpersonal) in nature.

According to this model, when an individual engages in NSSI it should serve one or more of the following four functions: (a) automatic-negative reinforcement (i.e., to reduce tension or another affective state); (b) automatic-positive reinforcement (i.e., to create a desirable physiological state); (c) social-positive reinforcement (i.e., to provide attention from others); and/or (d) social-negative reinforcement (i.e., to offer escape from interpersonal tasks or demands; Lloyd-Richardson et al., 2009). Each of these four dimensions is discussed in more detail below.

Automatic-Negative Reinforcement

This type of reinforcement refers to an individual's use of NSSI to stop or remove a particular and undesirable emotional or cognitive state, such as to release tension or to distract from disturbing or aversive thoughts (Lloyd-Richardson et al., 2009). Consequently, the reinforcement derived from the NSSI occurs in the form of escaping or avoiding aversive thoughts and/or feelings. As such, automatic functions serve to regulate an individual's own internal states.

Negative affect regulation is the function most often mentioned and described by theoretical and empirical reports (Lloyd-Richardson et al., 2009). A number of studies (e.g., Lloyd-Richardson, Perrine, Dierker, & Kelley, 2007; Nixon, Cloutier, & Aggarwal, 2002; Rodham, Hawton, & Evans, 2004; Ross & Heath, 2002) have provided strong empirical support for an automatic-negative reinforcement model of NSSI, with commonly endorsed reasons for NSSI suggested to include "to get out my frustrations," "to reduce emotional pain," "to express my anger toward others," and "to reduce tension" (Lloyd-Richardson et al., 2009). Among hospitalized youth, automatic-negative reinforcement is the function most frequently reported (Nixon et al., 2002; Nock & Prinstein, 2004) and is the only one of the four functions significantly related to suicide attempts (Nock & Prinstein, 2005).

Automatic-Positive Reinforcement

This refers to the use of NSSI to generate some desired internal state. For example, many youth who engage in NSSI report doing so to "just feel something" (Lloyd-Richardson et al., 2009). Among a clinical sample of adolescents, this was the model's second most endorsed function (Lloyd-Richardson et al., 2009), and individuals' endorsement of this function is strongest in the presence of symptoms of depression and posttraumatic stress disorder (Nock & Prinstein, 2005).

Social-Positive Reinforcement

In contrast to automatic functions, which involve regulation of internal states, social functions serve to regulate an individual's external environment. Social-positive reinforcement refers to the use of NSSI to gain attention or to access some particular social resource (Lloyd-Richardson et al., 2009). For example, the social-positive reinforcement function can be seen among youth reporting that they are engaging in NSSI "to let others know how I am feeling" and "to get my therapist to [react in a certain way]." Among a community sample of adolescents, youth who engaged in NSSI reported social-reinforcement motives almost as frequently as automatic-reinforcement motives (Lloyd-Richardson et al., 2007).

Social-Negative Reinforcement

This refers to the use of NSSI to escape from some interpersonal tasks or demands. Youth who report engaging in NSSI "to get out of going to school," "to get other kids or adults to leave me alone," or "to get my parents to stop fighting," are consistent with a social-negative reinforcement function of NSSI. Although research suggests that hospitalized adolescents appear to report social functions for NSSI less frequently than automatic functions, they do report the presence of social functions with some regularity, and among community samples social functions have been endorsed as frequently as automatic functions. In addition, endorsement of social functions is associated with the report of other social concerns by adolescents as well as with symptoms of depression (Lloyd-Richardson et al., 2009).

Although a functional model has the most empirical support as a causal mechanism for the development of NSSI, neither this model nor the others reviewed in this chapter are by themselves capable of accounting for the complex and multiply determined causes presumed to lead to NSSI. To more fully understand the causes of NSSI, it is therefore necessary to have an organizational framework that includes and integrates information from a variety of perspectives. One such framework is Walsh's (2006) biopsychosocial model of NSSI, which provides a highly useful, practical, and comprehensive conceptual foundation for understanding the causal variables of NSSI.

A Biopsychosocial Model of NSSI

In this model, NSSI is viewed as the result of a complex interaction between (a) environmental, (b) biological, (c) cognitive, (d) affective, and (e) behavioral dimensions. For the large majority of individuals, all five dimensions play an important role in the emergence and recurrence of NSSI, although the precise contribution of each dimension is unique for each individual (Walsh, 2006). For example, environmental and biological dimensions may play more important causal roles in some people, whereas for others cognitive, affective, or behavioral dimensions may predominate.

Environmental Dimension

According to Walsh (2006), the environmental dimension contributing to the occurrence of NSSI includes three basic categories: (a) family historical, (b) individual historical, and (c) current environmental elements.

Family Historical Elements

Family historical elements refers to key aspects of the history of the nuclear, extended, or surrogate family that have been observed, but not directly experienced (Walsh, 2006). For example, to observe suicidal behavior among members of one's family is different from being personally suicidal. Many family historical elements have been linked by research to the later development of NSSI in youth, including mental illness, suicide, substance abuse, violence, and self-injury in the family (D'Onofrio, 2007; Favazza, 1996, 1998; Walsh, 2006).

Family environments teach children behaviors through modeling, reinforcement, extinction, and punishment on a daily basis (Walsh, 2006). Further, children actively observe adult family members and frequently imitate them. When family members respond explosively and angrily to disappointment and frustration, a child may learn to behave this way as well or may exhibit the opposite behavior (e.g., markedly inhibited in emotional expression) depending on particular family and environmental circumstances. Likewise, when family members respond to distress by engaging in self-medication through the abuse of alcohol or drugs, children may acquire these behaviors (Walsh, 2006).

Walsh (2006) suggests that self-destructive behavior is a particularly ominous pattern of behavior in family environments. When family members model self-destructive behaviors such as NSSI or suicide attempts, it conveys a variety of unspoken messages to children, such as: "Life is overwhelmingly painful," or "Life is not worth living," or "Distress can be relieved by behaving self-destructively," or "Others cannot help my pain," or "My pain negates responsibilities I have to others." Unfortunately, children living with family members who engage in self-destructive behavior may come to consider NSSI as a viable option when faced with life challenges.

Individual Historical Elements

Individual historical elements include those in an individual's personal history that have been directly experienced rather than observed (Walsh, 2006). Although there are many examples of elements in an individual's history that may be associated with NSSI (e.g., death of parent or caregiver; loss through separation, divorce, or removal from the home), four of the most significant of these are (a) childhood adversities, (b) child maltreatment, (c) exposure, and (d) invalidating family environments.

Childhood adversities. The experience of trauma, particularly in childhood, frequently has a profound effect on psychological development and adaptive functioning in adolescence and correlates highly with NSSI (Conterio & Lader, 1998; Farber, 2000; van der Kolk, 2005; Yates, 2004). Childhood trauma, particularly sexual abuse, has received considerable investigation in the literature and has frequently been suggested as a primary factor in the initiation of self-destructive behaviors (Favazza, 1996; Noll, Horowitz, Bonanno, Trickett, & Putnam, 2003; Paivio & McCulloch, 2004). Other childhood adversities that have been found to raise risk considerably in youth include being the victim of a physical attack, parental loss or deprivation, traumatic medical or surgical procedures, and being an accident victim or witness to violence in general and family violence in particular (D'Onofrio, 2007; Walsh, 2006). These traumatic experiences can flood the vulnerable child with recurrent thoughts, images, or flashbacks, which in turn can raise emotionality and tension. Those individuals who engage in NSSI often report it offers the opportunity to achieve some measure of control of these thoughts and to release tension. However, recent research suggests that trauma does not play as large a role in the development of NSSI as was previously believed (Walsh, 2006).

Child maltreatment. A growing body of research has addressed a child's experience of "complex trauma" (i.e., a chronic history of emotional and physical maltreatment, neglect, or invalidating childrearing environments) and the etiology of NSSI (D'Onofrio, 2007; Linehan, 1993; van der Kolk, 2005). Child maltreatment exemplifies a toxic relational environment that poses significant risks for adaptation across biological, psychological, and interpersonal domains of development (Cicchetti & Toth, 2005). Children are particularly at risk for maltreatment if there is a history of alcoholism, mental illness, or suicide in the family (van der Kolk, 2005; Walsh, 2006).

Historically, many clinicians have suggested that trauma and the child maltreatment that typically causes it plays a central role in the development of NSSI (e.g., D'Onofrio, 2007; Favazza, 1998). Although child maltreatment can be a potential risk factor for the development of NSSI, recent research suggests that the relationship between child maltreatment and NSSI may be overstated because the two are correlated with similar psychiatric risk factors. For example, a recent meta-analysis found that the relationship between child sexual abuse (the most commonly cited form of child maltreatment linked to NSSI) and NSSI was relatively small, and that in studies that controlled for psychiatric risk factors, childhood sexual abuse explained little or no unique variance (Klonsky & Moyer, 2008). Moreover, Walsh (2006) has identified what he views as a "sub-group" of self-injurers who convincingly deny any history of physical or sexual abuse. As such, school practitioners should not assume that child maltreatment is a necessary precursor to NSSI. More information regarding the relationship between child maltreatment and NSSI is provided in Chapter 3.

Exposure. Adolescents are at increased risk to experiment with NSSI if they are exposed to such behavior through a sibling, peer, the media, or the Internet (Nock & Prinstein, 2005; Walsh, 2006; Whitlock, Powers, & Eckenrode, 2006). Unlike younger children, adolescents are more apt to use peers as models for social comparison and identity development. For some youth, NSSI behaviors may provide a potent social-positive reinforcement function, in that it may gain the attention and admiration of significant others that engage in risk-taking behaviors such as NSSI, substance abuse, or eating disorders (Lloyd-Richardson et al., 2009). There appears to be a powerful bond between self-injurers that fortifies group cohesiveness and appeals to vulnerable adolescents who want desperately to feel part of a group. For many of those who self-injure, the ability to find others like themselves reduces the isolation and loneliness that so often characterizes the behavior.

For others, however, active participation in online communities may substitute for the real work required to develop positive coping and healthy relationships (D'Onofrio, 2007; Whitlock, Lader, & Conterio, 2007). For example, there has recently been a tremendous increase in Web sites devoted to individuals who engaged in NSSI posted on the Internet (D'Onofrio, 2007). Unfortunately, although research suggests that online interactions can provide needed social support for otherwise isolated youth who engage in NSSI, they may also encourage, normalize, and promote this behavior. Further, some Internet sites may add potentially lethal behaviors to the repertoires of these students, increasing their risk for accidental death or suicide (Whitlock et al., 2006). More information on the topic of the Internet and its relationship to NSSI in youth is provided in Chapter 6.

Invalidating family environments. Linehan (1993), in describing the family environments of individuals with borderline personality disorder, contends that in many of these families the emotional experiences of children are often at best ignored and at worst denied, ridiculed, or condemned. These invalidating environments may also be widely experienced by youth engaging in NSSI, and often have severely deleterious effects. For example, invalidating family environments may potentially result in children questioning not only the accuracy, but also the very presence of their own internal feeling states (Walsh, 2006). Additionally, such environments may reinforce only the most extreme levels of emotional responses. As noted by Walsh (2006):

If a child indicates in a subtle manner that he or she is distressed, the invalidating environment may ignore the communication. Only when the child presents with an extreme emotional behavior (e.g., a tantrum) does he or she receive a response. The entire pattern is conducive to reinforcing maladaptive behavior while extinguishing adaptive behavior. When such a pattern is repeated countless times for many years, the end result can be an emotionally dysregulated person. Such people may come to rely on self-invalidating behaviors such as self-injury to manage emotional distress. (p. 60)

Current Environmental Elements

Adolescents are frequently subject to extraordinary pressures and many of these may precipitate tensions and elevate emotionality, which in turn creates the foundation for seeking relief, attention, or control through NSSI. These precipitating events may include loss (e.g., death, parental divorce, broken romance), peer conflicts or rejection, academic or disciplinary crises at school, and violent episodes or arguments with parents at home (Lieberman & Poland, 2006). According to Walsh (2006) individuals who have experienced aversive conditions in both their family and personal history may be particularly sensitive to similar problems occurring in the present. For example, a teenager who experienced loss of a parent or caregiver during childhood may be particularly reactive to losses in peer relationships that occur during adolescence. Or, an adolescent who was sexually or physically abused as a child may be extremely sensitive to threats of abuse in the present, even including normal and appropriate sexual behavior. Consequently, "the more complicated and aversive the individual's historical context, the more vulnerable he or she is likely to be in the present to negative experiences" (p. 62).

Biological Dimension

The relationship between biology and NSSI is a complex one. For example, a number of psychiatric conditions associated with NSSI have been shown to have biological components, including depression, bipolar disorder, schizophrenia, and borderline personality disorder. Moreover, there are several physiological problems commonly associated with NSSI, including physical illness (e.g., asthma, diabetes) and sleep disorders (Walsh, 2006). Although some research suggests there are biological differences between individuals who engage in NSSI and those who do not, little or no research has addressed this issue among adolescent populations. To date, the majority of the (adult) research that has addressed the biology of NSSI has been conducted with women with borderline personality disorder and, in the majority of cases, suicidal behavior and non-suicidal self-injury were not differentiated (Jacobson & Gould, 2007).

Despite these limitations, research does suggest that a number of biological variables may play a causal role in NSSI, including biological vulnerability to emotional dysregulation, limbic system dysfunction, serotonin level dysfunction, endogenous opioid system dysfunction, and diminished pain sensitivity (Walsh, 2006). For example, it has long been theorized that lower levels of serotonin are associated with NSSI (Favazza, 1996), and the effective use of selective serotonin reuptake inhibitors, or SSRIs (e.g., Prozac, Paxil, Zoloft, Lexipro) in reducing depression and self-injury in some individuals has provided some support for this hypothesis (Grossman & Siever, 2001). Additionally, the endogenous opioid system may not only be a key biological factor in the etiology of NSSI in youth, but may also play a central role in maintenance and repetition of it. Many adolescents report an absence of pain at the time of their self-injurious acts, and the powerful endorphin release initiated by NSSI may provide a biologically induced sense of euphoric relief or release. Similar to the tolerance developed to alcohol by individuals who consume it too frequently, repetitively engaging in self-injury often eventually results in the individual obtaining a tolerance to it, thus requiring an increase in frequency of NSSI to compensate (D'Onofrio, 2007; Grossman & Siever, 2001; Walsh, 2006). For more information on biological and neurobiological perspectives on NSSI, the reader is referred to Osuch and Payne (2009).

Cognitive Dimension

The cognitive dimension associated with NSSI corresponds with one of two basic categories: *cognitive interpretations of environmental events* and *self-generated cognitions*. The first category refers to the tendency by some individuals to engage in irrational thoughts and cognitive distortions in response to particular environmental events. For example, as noted by Walsh (2006), individuals who are victims of sexual abuse often engage in irrational thoughts focusing on self-blame (e.g., "I have should have done more to stop the abuse," or "I must have wanted it to happen since it went on so long"). There is considerable evidence that individuals high in self-derogation and self-blame are at increased risk for self-punishment and self-directed anger through NSSI (Klonsky, 2007; Klonsky & Glenn, 2009). Working with youth to relinquish such self-defeating and irrational cognitions is often a key element of effective treatment. However, it is important for those working with self-injuring youth to recognize that environmental events, even potentially traumatic ones, are problematic only if the person engaging in NSSI interprets them to be aversive, painful, or disorganizing (Walsh, 2006). Consequently, understanding the client's perceptions regarding particular environmental events is often as or more important than the events themselves.

The second major category of cognitive distortion is self-generated cognitions. In contrast to the external events and circumstances that may lead to the development of irrational thoughts described above, self-generated cognitions are triggered by internal cues (Walsh, 2006). These are thoughts that have no specific environmental causal triggers. For example, if an individual wakes up and thinks to himself, "Another day to feel awful; I wonder how I will get through it?" he is engaging in a self-generated cognition. The individual has just awakened; no particular environmental event has led to these thoughts – they are simply habitual, maladaptive patterns of thinking. Assessment of these recurring, negative, and irrational thoughts is essential and is discussed in greater detail in Chapter 6. Moreover, for effective treatment to occur, irrational cognitions need to be identified and modified – procedures that are discussed in greater detail in Chapter 7.

Youth who engage in NSSI also exhibit a wide variety of cognitions that may trigger their acts of self-harm, and identifying them is a key step in assessment and intervention. According to Walsh (2006), thoughts that often precede occurrences of NSSI include "I have to do something," or "I deserve this," or "I hate my body so much," or "This will show people that I'm really hurting," or "This is the *only* way to deal with this problem." Replacing such thoughts with more rational (and positive) thoughts is a critical step in getting youth to decrease and hopefully end their NSSI behaviors.

Affective Dimension

There is considerable support in the professional literature suggesting that individuals who engage in NSSI have significant problems with affect regulation (Conterio & Lader, 1998; Favazza, 1996; Fonagy, Gergely, Jurist, & Target, 2002; Yates, 2004). In other words, NSSI may be viewed as a maladaptive coping strategy designed to regulate and control an adolescent's emotions and to relieve tension (Gratz & Roemer, 2004; Linehan, 1993; Suyemoto, 1998), elevate and relieve overwhelming negative emotions (Briere & Gil, 1998; Klonsky, 2007), and communicate difficult to express psychological distress (Gratz, 2006). Although NSSI appears most often to be performed with the intent of alleviating negative affect, there is strong support for self-derogation and self-punishment functions as well. Youth who engage in NSSI identify a wide range of emotions as preceding their acts of self-harm, including anger, contempt, sadness, tension, guilt, shame, worry, and grief (Alderman, 1997; Conterio & Lader, 1998). However, it is important to recognize that the affective dimension of NSSI is closely linked to the cognitive dimension; emotions often emerge from the distorted, irrational, and frequently self-blaming, cognitions that precede them (Walsh, 2006). As such, emotions are generally of critical importance in the assessment and treatment of NSSI.

Behavioral Dimension

The behavioral dimension includes overt actions that occur right before, accompany, and follow NSSI. Typical behavioral antecedents include family or peer conflicts, failure at an activity, isolation, sexual behavior, substance abuse, or eating-disordered behavior (Walsh, 2006). This dimension also includes actions that set the stage for NSSI, such as choosing the physical location for self-injury, securing a location to prevent interruption, and selecting a method for inflicting NSSI. It is critical that school personnel determine the temporally distant and the more immediate antecedents to NSSI, as well as the consequences students receive for engaging in it. For example, after engaging in NSSI, some individuals fall asleep immediately afterward. Others may remain agitated and seek other forms of release, whereas some may return to normal activities. The consequences of engaging in NSSI provide a great deal of information regarding why this behavior is repeated; that is, what *function* it serves for the individual. Only after a thorough, individual, functional assessment has been completed can an effective treatment plan be developed and implemented. A more detailed discussion of the functional assessment of NSSI is provided in Chapter 6.

Integration of the Five Dimensions

Although descriptive information about self-injurers is abundant in the literature, the causal pathways that lead to NSSI have been poorly articulated (D'Onofrio, 2007). Walsh (2006) proposes that each of the dimensions discussed above do not function in isolation, but are entirely interrelated and even interdependent. For example, NSSI behaviors are theorized to result from disturbances in cognition and affect; negative thoughts fuel and amplify negative emotions, which potentially lead to a variety of maladaptive coping behaviors such as NSSI, alcohol and substance abuse, and other self-destructive behaviors. Conversely, there is evidence to suggest that recurrent traumatic experiences have sustained physiological effects, including changes in brain chemistry (van der Kolk, McFarlane, & Wiesaeth, 1996). Each of these five dimensions (i.e., environmental, biological, cognitive, affective, and behavioral) must be considered by school personnel if effective assessment and treatment of youth engaging in NSSI is to occur.

Concluding Comments

This chapter has explored NSSI as a multifaceted, multi-determined behavior that is the result of intricate and complex interactions. School personnel should have a thorough understanding of how the five dimensions described above contribute to the development of NSSI. These areas have important implications for assessment and treatment – issues that will be discussed in subsequent chapters. However, before discussing assessment and treatment issues the next chapter examines the prevalence of NSSI and some prominent psychiatric conditions associated with it.

Chapter 3
Prevalence and Associated Conditions

This chapter explores the prevalence rates of NSSI in youth. Additionally, a review of psychiatric conditions frequently associated with NSSI is provided, including suicide, mood and anxiety disorders, substance-related disorders, hostility/anger, eating disorders, dissociative disorders, and borderline personality disorder.

Prevalence Rates of NSSI in Youth: Issues and Challenges

Because the professional literature on NSSI is still emerging and relatively new, there has been wide variability and little consistency in the methodology designed to study it. For example, in community samples, prevalence rates of NSSI have been reported to be as low as 4% (Briere & Gil, 1998) and as high as 47% (Lloyd-Richardson, Perrine, Dierker, & Kelley, 2007), and even higher in clinical samples (Nock & Prinstein, 2004). When examining prevalence rates of NSSI, a number of methodological variables need to be considered, including definitional, measurement, setting, and sample selection issues (Heath, Schaub, Holly, & Nixon, 2009). These issues are discussed in greater detail below.

Definitional Issues

Many studies conducted to date have employed a definition of NSSI that includes any form of self-inflicted injury, including self-poisoning, jumping from heights, and drug overdose (DeLeo & Heller, 2004, Haavisto et al., 2005; Hawton, Fagg, Simkin, Bale, & Bond, 2000; Heath et al, 2009). As a result of the various definitions of what constitutes self-injury, reported prevalence rates have varied (Heath et al., 2009). For example, a recent study found a surprisingly high prevalence rate of 47% in a community sample of adolescents (Lloyd-Richardson et al., 2007), despite excluding suicide attempts. However, an examination of the behaviors in the study revealed that picking an area of the skin until it bleeds was included as a form of NSSI. When the behavior was limited to cutting/carving, burning, tattooing, and scraping and erasing skin (i.e., using an eraser to rub skin to the point of bleeding

D.N. Miller, S.E. Brock, *Identifying, Assessing, and Treating Self-Injury at School*,
Developmental Psychopathology at School, DOI 10.1007/978-1-4419-6092-4_3,
© Springer Science+Business Media, LLC 2010

or burning), the 12-month prevalence rate dropped to 28% (Lloyd-Richardson et al., 2007). Moreover, other studies may limit the behavioral definition to skin cutting and fail to include burning, self-hitting, and other behaviors that may be more common in males than females (Heath et al., 2009). As a result, how NSSI is conceptualized and defined in these studies leads to the reporting of highly diverse figures and significant difficulties in deriving accurate prevalence rates.

Measurement Issues

Complicating the definitional issue further is the confusion that may result by how NSSI is measured. Some behavioral "checklists" provide those being assessed with a variety of possible self-injurious behaviors they may have engaged in, whereas others are more open-ended and rely on an individual's interpretation of what should or should not be included (e.g., "Have you ever hurt yourself on purpose?"; Heath et al., 2009). Moreover, when assessed by anonymous survey rather than interview, different results are often obtained. For example, Ross and Heath (2002) asked 440 high school students if they had ever hurt themselves on purpose. In response to this questionnaire item, 21% of the student respondents indicated they hurt themselves on purpose at least once. However, from a follow-up interview this was suggested to be an overestimate and only 14% of all respondents were found to meet to the definition of NSSI proposed by the authors; the others stated they meant they had hurt themselves emotionally, had engaged in food restriction, or denied they meant the response. Consequently, an interview format can result in lower prevalence rates in part due to better (i.e., more precise) accuracy of measurement (Heath et al., 2009).

An additional measurement issue to consider is the time frame and frequency variables used for criterion purposes. The most common method for examining this issue is lifetime prevalence and single occurrence; that is, has the individual ever (at least once) engaged in NSSI in his or her lifetime. There are studies, however, that use time frames of "the past year," "the past six months," or "currently engaging in self-injury." Similarly, some studies have required that respondents engaged in NSSI at least 10 times to be counted, others more than three times, and still others have used the term "repetitive self-injury" rather than specifically describe how many episodes of the behavior are needed (Heath et al., 2009).

Setting Issues

In determining prevalence rates of NSSI among youth, it is important to know whether participants in studies were drawn from clinical or community settings. Clinical settings include inpatient hospitals, outpatient settings, emergency rooms, and a variety of health and mental health agencies and clinics. Although these settings vary, they share more commonalities than differences in comparison to community settings, which include schools, colleges, and general population settings (Heath et al., 2009). Moreover, there are more studies in some areas than in others, and these cut across various age ranges of the participants. In general, there are a number of studies of NSSI in young adults in clinical settings, a few of young adults in community settings, a limited number of adolescents in clinical settings, and only a handful involving adolescents in community settings, such as schools (Heath et al., 2009).

Sample Selection Issues

The sample selection procedures used in studies can also affect reported prevalence rates of NSSI. For example, different prevalence rates are found for samples of younger adolescents (ages 12–16) compared to older adolescents and young adults. Moreover, there are fewer studies that examine the prevalence of NSSI in adolescents as compared to young adults. As a result, some authors have relied on studies of young adults to draw conclusions regarding the prevalence of NSSI among adolescents. A second issue related to sample selection is the proportion of females to males. To date, the majority of studies in clinical settings have included a larger number of females than males, leading to conclusions about the frequency, type and functions of NSSI being largely based on the study of females (Heath et al., 2009).

Demographic Issues

Several demographic issues need to be considered when discussing the prevalence rate of NSSI in youth, including age of onset, geographical and cultural issues, clinic versus community samples, and gender issues. These are described below, along with a discussion of whether the prevalence rate of NSSI among youth is increasing and the implications of NSSI for school-based practitioners.

Age of Onset

Most studies indicate that the majority of youth who engage in NSSI begin between the ages of 13–15 (Muehlenkamp & Gutierrez, 2007; Ross & Heath, 2002; Sourander et al., 2006), although there is some evidence that a significant proportion of youth begin earlier (Heath et al., 2009). For example, Ross and Heath (2002) found in their study of high school students that 25% of the students who reported engaging in NSSI first engaged in it prior to age 12.

Geographic, Cultural, and Ethnic Issues

Current research suggests there is little variation in the behavior of youth who engage in NSSI across urban or suburban areas, or in other countries (Heath et al.,

2009). For example, Ross and Heath (2002) compared urban and suburban high schools and found no significant differences in student prevalence rates of NSSI; other researchers have reported similar results (Laye-Gindhu & Schonert-Reichl, 2005; Muehlenkamp & Gutierrez, 2004). There are currently too few studies in non-western countries to make any generalized conclusions about NSSI in youth across cultures (Heath et al., 2009). However, studies conducted in Japan (Izutsu et al., 2006), Australia (DeLeo & Heller, 2004) and Turkey (Zoroglu et al., 2003) reported prevalence rates of NSSI in the 10–20% range, which is generally consistent with the prevalence rates reported in the U.S. Studies of NSSI in less developed countries are lacking.

Community sample studies have reported some ethnic differences, with Caucasian youth being more likely to engage in NSSI than African-American youth (Muehlenkamp & Gutierrez, 2004, 2007; Whitlock, Eckenrode, & Silverman, 2006). Finally, although there are some indications that NSSI may occur more frequently in individuals who are gay, lesbian, or conflicted about their sexual orientation (Gratz, 2006; Heath et al., 2009; Whitlock et al., 2006), further study in this area is clearly needed before more definitive conclusions can be made.

Clinic-Based and Community-Based Prevalence Rates

Studies that have specifically examined the occurrence of NSSI in high school-aged youth indicate that between 15 and 20% will admit to having engaged in NSSI at least once (Laye-Gindhu & Schonert-Reichl, 2005; Muhlenkamp & Gutierrez, 2007; Nixon, Cloutier, & Aggarwal, 2002; Ross & Heath, 2002). As some of these studies were conducted in clinical settings rather than schools, they are very likely overestimates of actual prevalence rates among non-clinical youth. Research on NSSI, like other mental health problems, has consistently found prevalence rates to be higher in clinical settings than in community settings (Health et al., 2009). For example, Ross and Heath (2002), who have to date conducted the most direct investigation of NSSI in a community sample of adolescents, found that approximately 20% of the 440 high school students surveyed reported engaging in NSSI. However, follow-up interviews with these students indicated that 14% could be accurately described as engaging in NSSI.

Gender Issues

The issue of clinic versus community samples and the issue of gender differences would appear to be closely related. The significant gender difference of females outnumbering males that has been observed in clinical samples versus community samples appears largely due to two variables (Heath et al., 2009). First, females are more prone to seek help than males. Second, many clinical studies included participants whose method of self-harm included drug overdose or inappropriate ingestion of medication without suicidal intent – behaviors that have been found to occur more frequently in females than in males (Briere & Gil, 1998; Heath et al., 2009; Rodham, Hawton, & Evans, 2004). Although some recent studies have focused to a greater extent on males (e.g., Muehlenkamp & Gutierrez, 2007), most of the research on prevalence rates of NSSI to date has focused on clinical samples of young adult females. As such, there is a paucity of reliable epidemiological data providing a clear picture of the occurrence of NSSI among children and adolescents (D'Onofrio, 2007; Muehlenkamp, 2005). Although it appears likely that the number of adolescent females who engage in NSSI outnumber males (D'Onofrio, 2006; Walsh, 2006), research suggests that the level of these differences has perhaps been exaggerated (Heath et al., 2009).

Is the Prevalence of NSSI in Youth Increasing?

Although reports in the media suggest that NSSI is increasing among youth (e.g., D'Onofrio, 2007; Plener & Muehlenkamp, 2007; Walsh, 2006; Wilber, 2007), there are little empirical data that support this claim. Ironically, the increased media exposure given to NSSI may be one reason for this perceived increase among youth. Heath and colleagues (2009) suggest that the major reason for supporting the notion that NSSI is increasing among young people are studies of trends in "self-harm" conducted in the United Kingdom, which employ a much broader definition of NSSI that includes all non-fatal self-inflicted harm (e.g., drug overdose, suicide attempts). Moreover, comparing rates of youth NSSI with earlier prevalence rates is made difficult by the definitional and measurement problems previously described. It is also possible that rates of NSSI are made to appear to have increased due to increased disclosure of the condition among youth (Lieberman, Toste, & Heath, 2009), and the related possibility that youth are now more comfortable seeking help for NSSI than was the case in earlier decades (Heath et al., 2009).

Consistent with this last possibility was a study that found that the majority of health care providers from college and university counseling centers reported increases in help seeking for self-injuring behaviors over the previous 5-year period (Whitlock, Eels, Cummings, & Purington, 2009). As noted earlier, the topic of NSSI has also received much greater interest among various media outlets in recent years, which may also influence reports and identifications of NSSI (Heath et al., 2009). In sum, although there is some debate as to whether this increase is one of actual occurrence, increased disclosure, or a combination of the two (Lieberman et al., 2009), it is clearly the case that more students engaging in NSSI are coming to the attention of adults, including school personnel.

Implications for School-Based Practitioners

Although the issue of whether NSSI is actually increasing among youth is debatable, it is clear that this phenomenon is prevalent and one that has many important implications for school-based practitioners. First, because NSSI typically appears in early to mid-adolescence (i.e., ages 13–15 years), it is particularly important that middle and high school personnel be knowledgeable regarding NSSI. In addition, although NSSI is more typically associated with female than male adolescents, in part because females are more likely to seek help, practitioners should not make the erroneous assumption that boys are not engaging in NSSI. Males and females also differ in the methods they typically use when engaging in NSSI, with females more likely to engage in cutting themselves or overdosing without suicidal intent, and males more likely to hit themselves.

Although it has been suggested that non-heterosexual youth or adolescents struggling with their sexual identity may be at higher risk for engaging in NSSI, more research on the possible link between them is needed. School practitioners should be aware that the use of checklists and rating scales, although useful in the initial identification of students engaging in NSSI, will likely overestimate their prevalence. When using checklists and rating scales as screening devices, the use of follow-up interviews for identified youth is required, a topic that is discussed in greater detail in Chapter 6. Finally, for school personnel to adequately understand and respond to NSSI among students, they should have a clear understanding of other conditions associated with it, an issue that is discussed below.

Associated Conditions

One major criterion for obtaining diagnostic validity for a psychiatric phenomenon involves its distinctiveness from other disorders. As such, to adequately understand a condition such as NSSI it is necessary to have an understanding of other associated psychiatric conditions (Lofthouse, Muehlenkamp, & Adler, 2009). However, as mentioned in Chapter 1, NSSI is not currently listed as a disorder in the *DSM-IV-TR* (American Psychiatric Association [APA], 2000). Further, there has been much confusion and presumed overlap regarding such terms as "comorbidity," "co-occurrence," and "covariance," with many of these terms erroneously being used interchangeably within the professional literature. Consequently, research examining conditions associated with NSSI has been compromised from the lack of an accurate and consistent application of an operational definition, and the reader should be cognizant of this issue when considering conditions associated with NSSI (Lofthouse et al., 2009).

A second reason for the importance of understanding psychiatric conditions associated with NSSI is that the presence of multiple disorders leads to less positive outcomes and a more pessimistic prognosis than youth exhibiting only one disorder. As such, an associated disorder may be a possible risk factor for NSSI, and/or a developmental cause, consequence, or concomitant of NSSI.

Third, research on associated conditions is critical for knowing how to assess and treat NSSI in youth. Indeed, disregarding the occurrence of another condition may have significant implications for treatment recommendations and outcomes (Lofthouse et al., 2009). Finally, due to previous studies not sufficiently separating suicidal self-injury from non-suicidal self-injury, little is currently known about NSSI as defined in this book and its associated conditions during adolescence. However, what is known is discussed briefly below.

NSSI and Associated Psychiatric Disorders

NSSI has been associated with a wide variety of psychiatric disorders, although as noted earlier most of the studies published to date have failed to differentiate NSSI from suicidal self-injury. Lofthouse and colleagues (2009) recently conducted a review of the empirical literature on this topic and found only 15 published studies that specifically examined NSSI and associated psychiatric conditions in adolescent samples. Within inpatient samples, NSSI most frequently co-occurred with depression, followed by suicidal behavior, anxiety, substance abuse, eating disorders, and problems with anger/hostility. In outpatient samples, the most common co-occurring psychiatric problems included suicidal behavior followed by depression, anxiety, and substance abuse. In community samples, NSSI was most frequently associated with suicidal behavior, followed by depression, substance abuse, hostility/anger, and anxiety. Although other psychiatric disorders (e.g., borderline personality disorder) and conditions (e.g., trauma, child maltreatment) are commonly associated with NSSI, research suggests that their relationship may be more indirect and less substantial than previously believed.

The presence of one or more of these psychiatric problems may place youth at heightened risk for the development of NSSI. It is important to note, however, that in many cases NSSI is as least as likely to precede as follow the development of many of these problems. As such, school personnel should be cautious in making any assumptions about these disorders or conditions in terms of whether they contribute to or result from NSSI. As is frequently noted when examining comorbid psychological conditions, correlation does not imply causation. Below we discuss some of the most common psychiatric disorders or conditions associated with NSSI.

Suicide

The relationship between suicide and NSSI is complex and nuanced (Jacobson & Gould, 2007; Klonsky & Muehlenkamp, 2007). Suicide was found to be the condition most highly associated with NSSI in both outpatient and community samples, and to be second only to depression in inpatient samples (Lofthouse et al., 2009). A significant portion (50% in community samples; 70% of inpatient samples) of self-injurers report having attempted suicide at least once (Muehlenkamp & Gutierrez, 2007; Nock, Joiner, Gordon, Lloyd-Richardson, & Prinstein, 2006). However, it should be noted that although students who self-injure are at increased risk for suicide (Laye-Gindhu & Schonert-Reichl, 2005; Lloyd-Richardson et al., 2007), many are not suicidal and the functions of NSSI and suicide are frequently quite different (Miller & McConaughy, 2005). In fact, NSSI is counterintentional to suicide; the suicidal individual typically wants to end all feelings whereas the individual engaging in NSSI typically wants to feel better (D'Onofrio, 2007; Favazza, 1998). Consequently, most students who engage in NSSI appear to do so as a morbid, but effective, form of coping and self-help (Favazza, 1996).

Nevertheless, engaging in NSSI clearly places individuals at risk for a variety of suicidal behaviors, including suicidal ideation and suicide attempts (Jacobson & Gould, 2007). In particular, research has suggested that self-injurers are more likely to attempt suicide if they report being repulsed by life, exhibit greater apathy and self-criticism, have fewer connections to family members, and report less fear about suicide (Muehlenkamp & Gutierrez, 2004, 2007). Further, as noted in Chapter 2, individuals who engage in self-injury to escape or avoid the experience of highly distressful emotions are at increased risk for attempting suicide.

Joiner (2005, 2009) has suggested that engaging in NSSI may serve as "practice" for engaging in other potentially lethal behaviors such as suicide by desensitizing individuals to pain and habituating them to self-inflicted violence. Further, Gratz (2003) has theorized that individuals who engage in NSSI may become isolated, hopeless, and despairing as a result of it, which may lead them to become suicidal. There is also some evidence to suggest that adolescents who engage in both NSSI and suicide attempts are more impaired than those who do one or the other, and that these individuals may require more intensive treatment (Jacobson & Gould, 2007). Finally, Walsh (2006) has suggested that individuals who frequently engage in NSSI may eventually turn to suicide if and when their self-injury stops working as an effective affect management technique.

Given that engaging in NSSI places an individual at increased risk for suicide, it is critical that school-based mental health practitioners have a thorough understanding of youth suicidal behavior (Miller, in press; Miller & Eckert, 2009), including how to effectively assess (Brock, Sandoval, & Hart, 2006; Miller, in press; Miller & McConaughy, 2005) and intervene (Miller, in press; Sandoval & Zadeh, 2008) when students engage in suicidal ideation or make suicide attempts. Similarly, it is critical to routinely assess the intent or motivation underlying the self-injury, and to pay careful attention to the psychiatric symptoms being reported throughout treatment (Klonsky & Muehlenkamp, 2007). More information regarding how to screen for suicide risk and to effectively distinguish between NSSI and suicidal behavior is provided in Chapters 4 and 5.

Mood and Anxiety Disorders

Mood and anxiety disorders both constitute internalizing disorders, a class of disorders characterized by overcontrolled behavior and clinically significant levels of subjective distress (Merrell, 2008a). NSSI has been associated with mood disorders such as depression (Andover, Pepper, Ryabchenko, Orrico, & Gibb, 2005; Klonsky, Oltmanns, & Turkheimer, 2003; Ross & Heath, 2002) and the early onset of bipolar disorder (Hawton, Sutton, Haw, Sinclair, & Harriss, 2005). Anxiety disorders are also associated with NSSI (Ross & Heath, 2002), and there is some evidence that anxiety confers greater risk for skin cutting than other forms of NSSI (Andover et al., 2005; Klonsky & Glenn, 2009). A particular anxiety disorder associated with NSSI is posttraumatic stress disorder (PTSD), which involves a triad of defining symptoms following exposure to a traumatic experience (House, 1999, 2002; Nickerson, Reeves, Brock, & Jimerson, 2009; van der Kolk, 2005). The core symptoms of PTSD include (a) a recurrent re-experiencing of the stress; (b) persistent avoidance of reminders of the event and a decrease in general responsiveness (emotional numbing); and (c) persistent hyperarousal (APA, 2000).

Collectively, these core symptoms can create a foundation that might precipitate self-injurious impulses and behavior. Although it has been suggested that exposure to trauma is the factor most highly associated with NSSI (e.g., D'Onofrio, 2007), and trauma (and the PTSD that often results from it) is clearly associated with NSSI, not all youth who engage in NSSI have experienced trauma or PTSD (Walsh, 2006). Additionally, although youth who engage in NSSI may be diagnosed with a specific mood disorder such as major depression or bipolar disorder, not all youth who engage in NSSI meet full diagnostic criteria for these disorders. However, in many if not most cases, the presence of depressive and/or anxious symptoms is a prominent feature of youth who engage in NSSI (D'Onofrio, 2007).

Substance-Related Disorders

Like self-injury, substance abuse is typically conducted for the regulation of mood. Although some variability exists in terms of how substance abuse may occur in youth engaging in NSSI, a link between them has been established (Conterio & Lader, 1998; Walsh, 2006; Yates, 2004). Mood-altering substances such as drugs and alcohol are used in different ways by youth who engage in NSSI, and may pose differential risks depending on the nature and context of their use. For example, some youth may first engage in substance abuse to modulate their emotional states and engage in NSSI if and when this is no longer effective (D'Onofrio, 2007). The risk of lethal NSSI can also increase when substance abuse occurs. For example, youth engaging in NSSI who are also drinking heavily may pass out and die as a result of alcohol poisoning or blood loss, which may falsely create the appearance of suicide.

Hostility/Anger

The exhibition of hostile and angry behavior is associated with NSSI, although research suggests it is typically not as highly associated with it as other problems such as suicidal behavior, depression and anxiety, and substance abuse (Lofthouse et al., 2009). Students who exhibit extreme levels of anger and hostility may be exhibiting a conduct disorder (Hughes, Crothers, & Jimerson, 2008), which places them at risk for a host of other problems, including NSSI. Youth who exhibit hostile and angry behavior are often particularly difficult to treat.

Eating Disorders

Eating disorders include anorexia nervosa and bulimia. Anorexia nervosa is characterized by a refusal to maintain a minimally normal body weight, whereas bulimia nervosa is characterized by repeated episodes of binge eating followed by inappropriate compensatory behaviors such as self-induced vomiting, fasting, or excessive exercise (APA, 2000). Many researchers have found high rates of association between NSSI and eating disorders, ranging from 25% in some studies (Favaro, Ferrera, & Santonastoso, 2004; Sansone & Levitt, 2004) to 75% in clinical samples (Favazza, 1998; Muehlenkamp, 2005; Sansone & Levitt, 2004; Whitlock et al., 2006). It has been suggested that this high level of association may be due to the striking similarities between the two syndromes (D'Onofrio, 2007; Favazza, 1998). In particular, both appear more typically in females and begin during adolescence. Moreover, D'Onofrio (2007) suggests:

> ...both are linked to the felt sense of body dissatisfaction and need for self-punishment; both serve similar psychological functions in terms of regulating affect and experiencing emotional relief; and both function as maneuvers to reclaim control over one's life by taking possession and controlling one's own body. (p. 66)

Dissociative Disorders

A relationship between NSSI and dissociative disorders has also been proposed (Briere & Gil, 1998; Conterio & Lader, 1998), although little research has been conducted demonstrating a clear relationship between the two. There are five types of dissociative disorders (i.e., dissociative amnesia, dissociative fugue, dissociative identity disorder, depersonalization disorder, dissociative disorder not otherwise specified), although common to each of them is "a disruption in the usually integrated functions of consciousness, memory, identity, or perception" (APA, 2000, p. 519). Dissociative symptoms are included in the diagnostic criteria for PTSD, and it has been suggested among some clinicians that youth who engage in NSSI have frequently experienced some sort of trauma – often the result of a form of child maltreatment such as sexual or physical abuse, which then leads to the development of PTSD, dissociative disorders or symptoms, and to subsequent NSSI (e.g., D'Onofrio, 2007). Additionally, some youth who self-injure refer to a state of emotional "numbness" prior to the behavior, and claim that NSSI serves to stop or prevent dissociation from occurring. Although dissociative symptoms in children and youth are not uncommon, genuine dissociative disorders are very rare

(House, 1999, 2002). Moreover, except under highly unusual circumstances, school-based professionals conducting social-emotional assessments of student functioning (e.g., school psychologists) generally do not (and often should not) make these diagnoses.

Borderline Personality Disorder

Borderline personality disorder (BPD) is associated with NSSI more than any other psychiatric disorder (Alderman, 1997; D'Onofrio, 2007; Walsh, 2006). The essential feature of BPD is a "pervasive pattern of instability of interpersonal relationships, self-image, and affects, and marked impulsivity that begins by early adulthood and is present in a variety of contexts" (APA, 2000, p. 706). It is likely that the major reason for the association between BPD and self-injury is that engaging in NSSI is listed as one of the diagnostic criteria for BPD within the *DSM-IV-TR*. In fact, NSSI is listed as a diagnostic criterion only for this disorder. Because emotional dysregulation is considered a core feature of BPD, it is not surprising that BPD and NSSI are thought to be closely related by many mental health professionals (Klonsky & Glenn, 2009). However, the vast majority of youth who exhibit NSSI do *not* meet diagnostic criteria for BPD (Walsh, 2006), and school professionals are advised to use extreme caution about diagnosing an adolescent with a personality disorder, given that difficulty of accurately making this diagnosis, the controversy surrounding it, and its questionable utility (House, 1999, 2002).

Only one study to date has examined NSSI and BPD in adolescence. Nock and colleagues (2006) used structured diagnostic interviews to examine the relationship between NSSI and various *DSM-IV-TR* Axis I and Axis II disorders in a sample of 12–17-year-old psychiatric inpatients and found that 52% of their sample met diagnostic criteria for BPD. However, these researchers noted that this figure may be an overestimate because they were not able to examine the rate of BPD without filtering out the symptom of self-injury. In addition, given that this study was conducted with a clinic sample, it may overestimate the relationship between BPD and NSSI in a non-clinical, community-based sample. In another study conducted with adults where self-injurious behaviors were statistically controlled, only 29% met diagnostic criteria for BPD (Herpertz, Sass, & Favazza, 1997). In addition, Favazza and Rosenthal (1990) found that once self-injurious behavior stops, many individuals no longer meet diagnostic criteria for BPD.

Finally, as with the other psychiatric disorders associated with NSSI, it is not currently known whether NSSI typically develops before, after, or together with other BPD symptoms. Clearly, more longitudinal studies with adolescent samples are necessary to examine the relationship between BPD and NSSI among youth (Lofthouse et al., 2009; Nock et al., 2006).

Concluding Comments

Understanding the psychiatric conditions associated with NSSI has many important implications for school practitioners. Perhaps the most important is that the more psychiatric disorders a youth engaging in NSSI exhibits, the more challenging assessment and treatment typically becomes. In particular, school professionals, especially school-based mental health professionals, should understand the similarities and differences between NSSI and suicidal behavior in children and youth (Miller & McConaughy, 2005), particularly in the context of assessment. More information on this topic is provided in Chapter 5. Finally, an understanding of the psychiatric conditions associated with NSSI is essential for case finding, screening, and referral, which is the subject of Chapter 4.

Chapter 4
Case Finding, Screening, and Referral

The goal of this chapter is to provide school-based mental health professionals with information and guidance that will help to identify the possible presence of NSSI, and of the need for further psychological assessment and immediate treatment referrals. It begins with a discussion of the school-based mental health professional's roles and responsibilities in the identification of NSSI, then explores the specific risk factors and warning signs of these behaviors, and concludes with a discussion of the initial referral and screening of self-injury.

Roles and Responsibilities of School-Based Mental Health Professionals

School psychologists and other school-based mental health professionals can be expected to identify self-injury risk factors and warning signs, make appropriate referrals, and be familiar with the available treatment options (discussed further in Chapter 7). Although students may be referred for *IDEA* or 504 Plans (*Rehabilitation Act of 1973*) assessment due to a variety of emotional/behavioral problems that often co-exist with self-injury, the assessment of self-injury symptoms is often neglected because, as previously discussed, NSSI currently is not a specific *IDEA* special education eligibility category nor a *DSM-IV-TR* (American Psychiatric Association [APA], 2000) diagnostic classification, although it does appear it will be listed as a disorder in the next edition of the DSM. As a consequence of the fact that traditional classification/diagnostic schemes do not currently address self-injury per se, those who engage in NSSI may go unnoticed or be misidentified. This is problematic, as failure to identify these problems can lead to the persistence of maladaptive behavior into adulthood. School-based mental health professionals with knowledge of how to screen, assess, and make referrals for treatment of NSSI will be positioned to conduct the evaluation required to determine the needs of students with these challenging behaviors, and help guide students and their families toward appropriate services.

In addition to assessing individuals, a school-based mental health professional may lead school-wide prevention initiatives and advocate for more specialized

D.N. Miller, S.E. Brock, *Identifying, Assessing, and Treating Self-Injury at School*, Developmental Psychopathology at School, DOI 10.1007/978-1-4419-6092-4_4, © Springer Science+Business Media, LLC 2010 school-based intervention. Prevention may include psychoeducational programs designed to help potential caregivers (e.g., parents, teachers, and students themselves) identify the risk factors and warning signs of NSSI. The information included in this chapter may be helpful in the development of such programs.

Interventions may include short-term and long-term follow-up programs targeting students who self-injure. Schools are in a unique position to monitor students on a daily basis, conduct ongoing screening and identification, and provide information regarding various treatment options (e.g., mental health services at school; referrals to professionals who are specially trained to work with youth who self-injure). Figure 4.1 presents the process of identifying self-injury beginning with the first signs of a student exhibiting behavioral, emotional, or learning challenges (case finding) through the potential completion of a psychological evaluation. Chapters 5 and 6 provide a more in-depth discussion of the assessment and evaluation process of NSSI in the school setting.

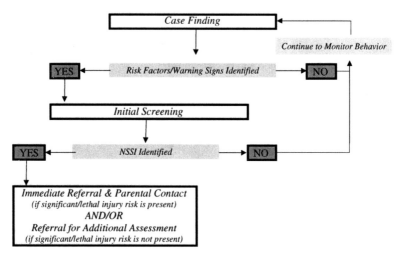

Fig. 4.1 This flowchart illustrates the process of initially identifying and screening for NSSI in the school setting

Risk Factors

Risk factors are variables that increase the odds of a disorder being manifested (Klonsky & Glenn, 2009). Although not perfect predictors, the presence of risk factors should direct attention toward the possible presence of warning signs, which may be the concrete manifestations of self-injurious behaviors. Risk factors (i.e., historical factors operating in the individual's past) that increase the odds of developing NSSI include demographics, child abuse, other forms of self-harm, dysfunctional family dynamics, having a friend who self-injures, psychiatric disturbances, and psychological factors.

Demographics

The available literature suggests a variety of demographic variables have varying degrees of association with NSSI. The specific factors considered in this section are gender, age, socioeconomic status, and ethnic, racial, and cultural background.

Gender. Shapiro's (2008) review suggested that girls self-injure more often than boys. However, some recent studies have reported similar rates for men and women, with the main gender difference being method of NSSI. Specifically, it has been suggested that although women are more likely to cut themselves, men are more likely to hit or burn themselves (Klonsky & Muehlenkamp, 2007).

Age. One of the most basic risk factors for NSSI is age. This pattern of behavior typically emerges in early adolescence (around 13–14 years; Klonsky, 2007; Shapiro, 2008), although it may appear somewhat earlier (11 or 12 years).

Socioeconomic status. Very little research has been conducted regarding the relationship between NSSI and socioeconomic status (Shapiro, 2008). However, Engstrom, Diderihsen, and Leflamme (2004) suggest that lower socioeconomic status may be a risk factor. Specifically, they report that among 10–19-year-olds in Sweden, having parents who were unskilled manual workers and, in particular, being from a family that received welfare benefits increased the odds of a youth engaging in NSSI.

Ethnic, racial, and cultural background. Klonsky and Muehlenkamp's (2007) review identifies "striking patterns" (p. 1047) of NSSI among ethnic groups, with rates of NSSI higher among Caucasians than among non-Caucasians. However, their review acknowledged that this link has not been consistently supported by empirical research. Further, Hilt, Cha, and Nolen-Hoeksema (2008) failed to find any differences between ethnic (Hispanic vs. non-Hispanic) or racial (Caucasian vs. African-American) groups. Shapiro's (2008) review suggests that there is no conclusive evidence of a link between culture and NSSI.

Child Abuse

Retrospectively reported childhood abuse (in particular sexual abuse) is associated with NSSI during adolescence (Glassman, Weierich, Hooley, Deliberto, & Nock, 2007; Shapiro, 2008; Walsh, 2006; Weierich & Nock, 2008). However, as discussed in the previous chapter, this association is far from perfect and it cannot be assumed that all or even most youth who engage in self-injurious behaviors have been abused (Klonsky & Muehlenkamp, 2007). For example, Klonsky and Moyer (2008), who reviewed aggregated results from 43 studies, found only a modest relationship between child sexual abuse and NSSI. From this review, Klonsky and Glenn (2009) suggest that sexual abuse and self-injury might be correlated because they are associated with similar psychiatric risks and not because there is a causal connection between these two variables.

Self-Harm History

Janis and Nock (2008) suggest that when it comes to predicting the likelihood of future self-injurious behavior, considering prior behavior may be the best way to anticipate future behavior. In addition to a history of NSSI, other self-harm behaviors are also common in the backgrounds of youth who are self-injurers. Specifically, adolescents who engage in NSSI were more likely to have smoked cigarettes and used drugs compared to adolescents who did not self-injure (Hilt, Nock, Lloyd-Richardson, & Prinstein, 2008). Moreover, a history of unhealthy eating habits (e.g., bingeing and fasting) and eating disorders are more common among youth who self-injure as opposed to those who do not self-injure (Ross, Heath, & Toste, 2009). Other self-harm behaviors that may be associated with NSSI include a variety of risk-taking behaviors and self-medication (FirstSigns, 2008a).

Family Dynamics

Family dysfunction has been suggested to be a risk factor for NSSI (Crowell, Beauchanie, Smith, Vasilev, & Stevens, 2008). For example, having a family history that includes alcohol and drug abuse, and/or other self-destructive behaviors, increases the risk for NSSI (Shapiro, 2008). Supporting the observation that family dysfunction is associated with self-injury is the finding that the families of youth who self-injure exhibit less positive and more negative affect and have less cohesiveness when compared to the families of youth who do not self-injure. Further, youth who self-injure have been reported to display more opposition and defiance, and lower levels of positive emotions during conflict situations when compared to youth who do not self-injure (Crowell et al., 2008). Considering the literature as a whole, Klonsky and Glenn (2009) concluded that

> ...self-injurers report a lower quality of family environment compared to non-self-injurers; at the same time, not all self-injurers are distinguished by a poor family environment, and there is no evidence that family variables play a causal role in the development of [self-injury] (pp. 47–48).

Peer Modeling

There is some evidence to suggest that social modeling may play a role in, and increase the risk of, NSSI. Specifically, Nock and Prinstein (2005) found that just over 82% of one sample of self-injuring adolescents reported these same behaviors among at least one of their friends in the previous year.

Psychiatric Disturbance

As noted previously, NSSI appears only once in the *DSM-IV-TR* as a symptom of borderline personality disorder (APA, 2000, p. 710, criterion 5). Given this fact, it is not surprising that individuals who engage in self-injurious behavior demonstrate more symptoms of borderline personality disorder than do individuals who do not self-injure (Andover, Pepper, Ryabchenko, Orrico, & Gibb, 2005; Klonsky & Glenn, 2009). Although not included as a *DSM-IV-TR* symptom of other psychiatric disorders, as noted in Chapter 3 it is well established that self-injury is associated with a variety of other mental health challenges, and that the presence of mental illness increases the risk for NSSI. For example, suicidal behavior as well as symptoms of anxiety and mood disorders are associated with NSSI, as are eating disorders (e.g., anorexia nervosa, bulimia nervosa) and substance abuse (Andover et al., 2005; Klonsky & Glenn, 2009; Klonsky, & Muehlenkamp, 2007; Shapiro, 2008).

Psychological Factors

Finally, there are a variety of psychological variables which, when present, appear to increase the risk of NSSI. Some of these factors include the possible presence of dissociative behaviors, poor stress tolerance, deficits in social problem solving, negative emotionality, and negative self-image.

Dissociative behaviors. In a recent study of over 4,000 Finnish adolescents (ages 13–18 years) Tolmunen and colleagues (2008) investigated the relationship between dissociation and NSSI. Study results suggested high scores on a measure of dissociative experiences was a risk factor for self-injury. Further, they found that youth engaged in self-cutting had higher levels of dissociative experiences than did youth who engaged in other forms of self-injury. However, school personnel should understand that dissociative *experiences* are not identical to dissociative *disorders*. As discussed in Chapter 3, the number of youth who exhibit genuine dissociative disorders is quite small, and the relationship between NSSI and dissociative disorders is not as strong as was previously believed.

Poor stress tolerance. Relative difficulty dealing with stressful situations may also be a risk factor for NSSI. Supporting this observation are the results of a recent causal-comparative study of adolescents (ages 12–19 years). In this study, Nock and Mendes (2008) induced distress among participants by giving high levels of negative feedback regarding performance on a psychological test (regardless of participant test response, the experimenter told them that they had responded incorrectly to a predetermined series of test items). In response to the distress generated by the perception of responding incorrectly to test items, participants in a group of individuals who self-injured ($n = 62$) chose to stop taking the test significantly sooner than did a carefully matched control group of individuals who did not self-injure ($n = 30$). From this finding it was suggested that individuals who self-injure have less ability to tolerate distress. Further, this study documented higher levels of physiological hyperarousal (skin conductance) in the group of individuals who self-injure ($n = 62$), as compared to the control group of individuals who did not self-injure ($n = 30$). Nock and Mendes suggest that these findings may shed some light on the experiences that may be driving NSSI, and that addressing distress tolerance may be important to the treatment of self-injury.

Deficits in social problem solving. Poor social problem-solving skill may also be a risk factor for NSSI. Data in support of this observation can be found in the same study described above, which suggested individuals who self-injure have deficits in specific social problem-solving skills (Nock & Mendes, 2008). Results of an experimenter-developed social problem-solving test (which asks for questions about specific social scenarios) revealed that the self-injury group was more likely to select negative (or maladaptive) solutions to social problems than the control group. In addition, the self-injury group rated their ability to adaptively perform solutions lower than the control group.

Negative emotionality. Klonsky and Muehlenkamp's (2007) review reports that individuals who self-injure "experience more frequent and intense negative emotions in their daily lives than individuals who do not self-injure" (p. 1047). For example, in a group of individuals with bulimia nervosa, increases in negative and decreases in positive affect were reported to occur prior to an act of NSSI (Muehlenkamp et al., 2009). Not only can the presence of negative emotions be considered a risk factor for NSSI, the function of self-injurious behaviors frequently includes the reduction of these negative emotions (Klonsky, 2007). Klonsky and Muehlenkamp's (2007) review also reports that self-injurers "display difficulties with their experience, awareness, and expression of emotions" (p. 1047).

Negative self-image. It has been suggested that individuals with a poor self-image are at risk for NSSI, and in fact Klonsky (2007) has reported such negative self-perceptions (and associated self-punishment) to be functions of self-injurious behaviors. Self-criticism may be an important mediator in the relationship between emotional abuse and NSSI (Glassman et al., 2007). Further, Klonsky and Glenn (2009) reported that "individuals high in *both* emotion dysregulation and self-derogation are at particular risk for self-injury, although research has not yet explicitly addressed the combination of these characteristics in relation to self-injury risk" (p. 50).

Self-Injury Warning Signs

Although risk factors increase the odds of NSSI being manifested, they are far from perfect predictors of these behaviors. While some students may have many risk factors, they may never engage in self-injury. Conversely, other students may have few or no risk factors and nevertheless engage in NSSI. Consequently, while educators need to be especially attentive for self-injury warning signs among students at risk for these behaviors (e.g., among special education students), they should also be vigilant for them within the general student population. Another important distinction between risk factors and warning signs is that risk factors can be operating in an individual's past (i.e., historical factors), whereas warning signs are always operating in the present (i.e., current factors). Warning signs that signal the possible presence of NSSI include both behavioral and physical signs.

Behavioral Warning Signs

Student behavior that may indicate a student is experiencing the kind of distress associated with NSSI includes other forms of self-destructive behavior, such as substance abuse. In addition to being risk factors, emotional negativity, general signs of depression, and poor self-esteem may also be considered warning signs for NSSI (FirstSigns, 2008b; Lieberman, Toste, & Heath, 2009). For example, the student known to be engaging in drug use and exhibiting an eating disorder may also be engaging in NSSI (Hilt et al., 2008; Lieberman et al., 2009; Ross et al., 2009). Similarly, the student who is currently demonstrating negative emotionality and negative self-esteem may also be demonstrating the behavioral warning signs of NSSI (Glassman et al., 2007; Klonsky, 2007; Klonsky & Muehlenkamp, 2007; Muehlenkamp et al., 2009).

Lieberman and colleagues (2009) also suggest that gun-play, risky sexual practices, running into traffic, and jumping from high places may be warning signs. Similarly, possession of objects that could be used for cutting (e.g., razors, broken glass, thumb tacks) may also be warning signs. A sudden change in peer group and/or withdrawal from prior relationships (or social isolation) has also been suggested to be a warning sign (Cleveland Clinic, 2009; FirstSigns, 2008a; 2008b; Lieberman et al., 2009). Finally, secretive behaviors, such as spending atypical amounts of time in the restroom or isolated areas in school or elsewhere, might also be a potential warning sign of NSSI (Lieberman et al., 2009).

Physical Warning Signs

The physical warning signs that NSSI may be occurring include cuts, scratches, or burns that do not appear to be accidental; reports of frequent "accidents" that have caused physical injury; frequently bandaged wrists and/or arms; a reluctance to take part in activities (e.g., physical exercise) that require a change of clothing; and the constant wearing of pants and long-sleeved shirts, even in hot weather (Cleveland Clinic, 2009; FirstSigns, 2008a; Lieberman et al., 2009). The direct observation of self-injurious behaviors such as self-punching or scratching, needle sticking, head banging, eye pressing, finger or arm biting, pulling out hair, or picking at skin are obvious warning signs.

Case Finding

Given the demographic data provided above, all middle and high schools should have staff training regarding the identification of risk factors and warning signs of NSSI. For schools to effectively identify potential NSSI symptoms, school staff must know *how* to refer and to *whom* to refer the student when they have concerns. This can be done through an in-service workshop, presentations at a staff meeting, and/or disseminating written materials that describe the risk factors and warning signs. In most schools, mental health professionals do not have the daily contact with students that other educators have and may be the first adults to recognize NSSI (Lieberman et al., 2009). Consequently, providing some form of staff development for all school staff members is essential (Nickerson, Reeves, Brock, & Jimerson, 2009). The "dos" and "don'ts" list developed by Lieberman and colleagues (2009) and provided in Table 4.1 can be used as a part of such training. In addition, the FirstSign.org.uk materials, such as the factsheets developed for parents/caregivers (2008a) and teachers (2008b), might be helpful resources in these staff development efforts.

Table 4.1 Suggestions for teachers: Helping youth who self-injure

Do:
- Try to approach the student in a calm and caring way.
- Accept him or her even though you may not accept the behavior.
- Let the student know howmuch you care about him or her and believe in his or herpotential.
- Understand that this is his or her way of coping with the pain he or she feels inside.
- Refer that student to your school-based professional (e.g., psychologist or counselor).
- Offer to go with that student to see the professional helper.
- Listen! Allow the student to talk to you. Be available.
- Discover what the student's personal strengths are and encourage him or her to use those strengths.
- Help him or her get involved in some area of interest (club, sport, or peer program).

Don't:
- Say anything to cause the student to feel guilt or shame (e.g., "what did you do to yourself?").
- Act shocked or appalled by his or her behavior.
- Talk about the student's [self-injury] in front of the class or around his or her peers.
- Try to teach the student what you think he or she should do.
- Judge the student, even if you do not agree with him or her.
- Tell the student that you won't tell anyone if he or she shares information about self-injuring behaviors with you.
- Use punishment or negative consequences if a student does self-injure.
- Make deals in an effort to get the student to stop.
- Make promises to the student that you can't keep.

Note. From Lieberman et al. (2009). Copyright © 2009 by Taylor & Francis Group. Reprinted with permission.

Another important group to train to recognize and appropriately respond to NSSI warning signs is students. Often times there is a "code of silence" among students; thus, case finding efforts need to teach students that seeking support for each other is not "tattling." Many schools have included instruction regarding risk factors and warning signs of mental health problems into health classes, with a special emphasis on *how* to refer and to *whom* to refer a friend when they recognize concerns

(Nickerson et al., 2009). The FirstSigns.org.uk (2008c) factsheet for friends might be an especially helpful resource for these educational efforts.

Initial Referral and Screening

School personnel interested in finding published, readily available curricula to assist in screening students for the possible presence of NSSI currently have very few options. One of the few published programs currently available is the *Signs of Self-Injury Prevention Program*, which is designed to address the issue of self-injury with high school student populations. Based on the same model as the similar *Signs of Suicide* (SOS) Program, the *Signs of Self-Injury Prevention Program* is designed to teach students how to recognize the signs of possible NSSI, either in themselves or others, and respond effectively if necessary by using the ACT approach (Acknowledge, Care, and Tell). A recent study (Muehlenkamp, Walsh, & McDade, in press) conducted with 274 high school students found that the program increased accurate knowledge and improved help-seeking attitudes and intentions among the student participants, and that it did not produce iatrogenic effects (i.e., inadvertent, negative effects). No significant changes were found regarding self-reported help-seeking behaviors as a result of the program. Although more research on this program is needed, preliminary evidence suggests it may be an effective program for screening and prevention in schools.

A protocol provided by Lieberman and colleagues (2009) can help to structure a school's approach to the initial referral and screening of students who self-injure. This protocol begins with staff development efforts. Consistent with the guidance offered by Davis and Sandoval (1991) regarding suicidal ideation, the protocol also recommends that all schools identify a designated reporter to whom all reports of youth suspected to be engaging in NSSI are brought. Specific instructions for making the referral to a designated reporter include guidance that a chain of supervision be maintained. Next, the protocol recommends an initial screening assessment be conducted by a school-based mental health professional (e.g., school psychologist or counselor).

When conducting the initial NSSI screening, it is essential that the screener remain calm and non-judgmental. Because the topic of self-injury is viewed by most people in the dominant culture as being surrounded by stigma and taboo, it will not be surprising for students engaging in these behaviors to feel that there are few if any caring adults who they can talk to openly and directly about these behaviors. Consequently, it is essential that the professional providing the initial screening assessment are attentive to Lieberman and colleagues' (2009) "dos" and "don'ts" list provided in Table 4.1.

According to Heath and Nixon (2009), the initial screening of the student for whom case finding efforts have identified risk factors and/or warning signs of NSSI should at a minimum include (a) a suicide risk assessment, (b) an injury risk assessment, and (c) some consideration of common co-occurring mental health challenges.

Suicide Risk Assessment

Although the incidence of NSSI and co-occurring suicide attempts is not clear, it is well established that many individuals who engage in NSSI do at some point in their lives engage in suicidal behavior as well (Lofthouse, Muehlenkamp, & Adler, 2009). Given this fact, and the reality that the presence of suicidal behaviors will complicate the response to self-injury (i.e., it will necessarily call for much more immediate interventions and parental contact), the initial screening of NSSI should always begin with a suicide risk assessment.

It is possible to efficiently and briefly (in less than 15 min) screen an individual for suicide risk (Gutierrez, Osman, & Kopper, 2000), and there are standardized screening tools available that can facilitate such screening efforts (e.g., the *Suicidal Ideation Questionnaire*; Reynolds, 1988). These screenings rarely yield false negatives, but will frequently yield false positives (i.e., they will frequently over-identify students as being potentially suicidal).

Risk assessment should begin by first discussing the reason for referral with the referring staff member and then working to establish rapport with the student (Brock, Sandoval, & Hart, 2006). The first step in the risk assessment process is to verify the presence of suicidal ideation. Once the student has been engaged (via demonstrations of empathy, respect, and warmth), he or she should be calmly but directly asked about the presence of suicidal intent. In doing so, it is important for the screener to be both direct and non-judgmental in his or her manner of questioning. For example, the screener might ask: "Sometimes when people have had your experiences and feelings they have thoughts of suicide. Is this something that you're thinking about?" (rather than asking, for example, "You are not thinking of hurting yourself, are you?"). If thoughts of suicide are not present, the initial screening can move directly to an examination of the seriousness of the student's NSSI. If thoughts of suicide are present, then additional suicide risk assessment questions will need to be asked.

From the work of Brock and colleagues (2006), Poland (1989), and Ramsay, Tanney, Lang, and Kinzel (2004), Fig. 4.2 provides a *Suicide Risk Assessment Summary Sheet* that can be used as a checklist to guide the risk assessment process. The items on this list are offered in order of importance to the assessment of suicide risk. The first and most important questions address factors operating in the present, and begin with direct inquiry about the presence of a suicide plan (e.g., "Do you have a plan for how you might act on your thoughts of suicide?"). In general, the greater the planning, the greater is the risk for suicide. Other specific questions to ask include: (a) "How might you do it?" (b) "How soon are you planning on suicide?" and (c) "Do you have access to means of attempt?" Next, the risk assessment involves direct inquiry about the degree to which the student is

Instructions: When a student acknowledges having suicidal thoughts, use the following form as a checklist to help assess suicide risk. Items are listed in order of importance.

	Risk present, but lower	Medium Risk	Higher Risk
1. Current Suicide Plan			
A. Details	☐ Vague	☐ Some specifics	☐ Well thought out
B. How prepared	☐ Means not available	☐ Has means close by	☐ Has means in hand
C. How soon	☐ No specific time	☐ Within a few days or hours	☐ Immediately
D. How (Lethality of method)	☐ Pills, slash wrists	☐ Drugs/alcohol, car wreck	☐ Gun, hanging, jumping
E. Chance of intervention	☐ Others present most of the time	☐ Others available if called upon	☐ No one nearby; isolated
2. Pain	☐ Pain is bearable	☐ Pain is almost unbearable	☐ Pain is unbearable
	☐ Wants pain to stop, not desperate	☐ Becoming desperate for relief	☐ Desperate for relief from pain
	☐ Identifies ways to stop the pain	☐ Limited ways to cope with pain	☐ Will do anything to stop the pain
3. Resources	☐ Help available; student acknowledges significant others are concerned/available to help	☐ Family and friends available, but are not perceived by the student to be willing to help	☐ Family and friends are not available and/or are hostile, injurious, exhausted
4. Prior Suicidal Behavior of…			
A. Self	☐ No prior suicidal behavior	☐ One previous low lethality attempt; history of threats	☐ One of high lethality, or multiple attempts of moderate lethality
B. Significant Others	☐ No significant others have engaged in suicidal behavior	☐ Significant others have recently attempted suicide	☐ Significant others have recently committed suicide
5. Mental Health	☐ History of mental illness, but not currently considered mentally ill	☐ Mentally ill, but currently receiving treatment	☐ Mentally ill and not currently receiving treatment
A. Coping behaviors	☐ Daily activities continue as usual with little change	☐ Some daily activities disrupted; disturbance in eating, sleeping, and schoolwork	☐ Gross disturbances in daily functioning
B. Depression	☐ Mild; feels slightly down	☐ Moderate; moody, sad, irritable, lonely, decrease of energy	☐ Overwhelmed with hopelessness, sadness, and feelings of helplessness
C. Medical status	☐ No significant medical problems	☐ Acute, but short-term, or psychosomatic illness	☐ Chronic debilitating, or acute catastrophic, illness
D. Other Psychopathology	☐ Stable relationships, personality, and school performance	☐ Recent acting-out behavior and substance abuse; acute suicidal behavior in stable personality	☐ Suicidal behavior in unstable personality; emotional disturbance; repeated difficulty with peers, family, and teacher
Total Checks			

Fig. 4.2 Suicide risk assessment summary sheet

currently experiencing psychological pain and the degree to which it is endurable (e.g., "Does your physical and/or emotional pain feel unbearable?"). In general, the more unbearable the pain, the greater is the risk. Another circumstance to be considered is the presence or absence of individuals who may be able to prevent the student from suicide. This will involve direct questioning about the possibility of rescue. The more isolated or "alone" the student reports to be, the greater is the risk.

In addition to addressing current factors, it is also recommended that historical variables be considered when conducting a suicide risk assessment. Specifically, it would be important to directly inquire about the student's history of suicidal behavior (e.g., "Have you or anyone close to you ever attempted suicide before?"). The more frequent the prior suicidal behavior, the greater the risk. In addition, it would be important to ask about the student's mental health history (e.g., "Have you ever had mental health care?"). The presence of mood disorders (especially bipolar disorder), schizophrenia, alcohol and substance abuse, trauma, and borderline personality disorder would be particular concerns. A more extensive discussion of variables to consider in differentiating NSSI from suicidal behavior is provided in Chapter 5.

As illustrated in Fig. 4.1, to the extent that the suicide risk assessment identifies suicidal behaviors (i.e., suicidal ideation; suicide attempts), a more or less immediate referral to a mental health professional and parental contact is indicated. However, to the extent that suicidal thoughts are not present, the initial screening of NSSI should proceed to the evaluation of the severity of the physical injuries.

Evaluation of Physical Injury

Next, the initial screening of NSSI should examine the severity of the student's physical injuries. The *How I Deal With Stress* questionnaire, developed by Heath and Nixon (2009) and offered in Fig. 4.3, can facilitate this examination. As high-lighted by Heath and Nixon, the importance of such evaluation is emphasized by the fact that even in the absence of risk for suicidal behaviors, the specific type

---

Please begin by completing the following information:

Age:_____   Sex: ☐ Male   ☐ Female
What **languages** do you speak at home? _____

Young adults have to deal with a lot of stress. In a recent survey, young adults said they used the following list of strategies to help them deal with problems. We are interested in knowing if you have also used any of these strategies to help you deal with stress.

Please read each item and indicate whether you:
      never used this strategy (0)
      used this strategy **only once** (1)
      used this strategy a **few times** to cope with stress (2)
      frequently used this strategy to cope with stress (3)

➢ Please note that some items are printed in **bold**. If you answer that you have used a bolded strategy (once, a couple of times, or frequently), please fill out the follow-up questions at the end of the survey.

Coping strategies		Never	Once	Few times	Frequently
1.	Try not to think about it	0	1	2	3
2.	Spend time alone	0	1	2	3
3.	Go out	0	1	2	3
4.	Talk to someone	0	1	2	3
5.	Try to solve the problem	0	1	2	3
6.	Do something to keep myself busy	0	1	2	3
7.	Say it doesn't matter	0	1	2	3
8.	Listen to music	0	1	2	3
9.	Exercise	0	1	2	3
10.	Play sports	0	1	2	3
11.	Read	0	1	2	3
12.	Go shopping	0	1	2	3
13.	Eat	0	1	2	3
14.	Stop eating	0	1	2	3
15.	Drink alcohol	0	1	2	3
16.	Hit someone	0	1	2	3
17.	Get into an argument with someone	0	1	2	3
18.	Do drugs	0	1	2	3
19.	Smoke	0	1	2	3
20.	Do risky things	0	1	2	3
21.	Physically hurt myself on purpose	0	1	2	3

Fig. 4.3 (continued)

22.	Cry	0	1	2	3
23.	Sleep	0	1	2	3
24.	Pray or engage in other religious	0	1	2	3
25.	Other: _____	0	1	2	3

"Talk to someone"
Please fill out this section if you answered that you indicated that you have used this strategy.

Who do you talk to? (circle all that apply)

Parents   Other family members   Friends
Romantic partner   Teachers   Other (specify) _____

How helpful is this strategy? (circle one)
0 – Never helpful
1 – Sometimes helpful
2 – Usually helpful
3 – Always helpful

"Do risky things"
Please fill out this section if you answered that you indicated that you have used this strategy.

What kind of risky activities have you engaged in? (circle all that apply)

Reckless Driving   Uncontrolled alcohol abuse   Drug abuse
Theft   Promiscuous/unprotected sex   Vandalism
Excessive gambling   Other (specify) ——————————————

How did the risky activities make you feel?

"Physically hurt myself on purpose"
Please fill out this section if you answered that you indicated that you have used this strategy.

Please circle any way that you have intentionally hurt yourself (without suicidal intent)

1. Cut your writs, arms or other areas of your body
2. Burned yourself
3. Scratched yourself, to the extent that scarring or bleeding occurred
4. Banged your head against something, to the extent that you caused a bruise to appear
5. Punched yourself, to the extent that you caused a bruise to appear

How old were you when your fist hurt yourself on purpose?   _____

When was the last time your hurt yourself on purpose?   _____

Fig. 4.3 (continued)

of NSSI being engaged in may place the student as risk for severe injury or even death.

Identified as "the brief screening measure of choice" by Cloutier and Humphreys (2009, p. 133), the *Self-Harm Behavior Questionnaire* (SHBQ; Gutierrez, Osman, Barrios, & Kopper, 2001) is a reliable and valid assessment tool that may be

How many years have you been hurting yourself on purpose? (If you are no longer doing this, how many years did you do this before you stopped?)   _____

Think of the longest period in which you engaged in self-injury (this could be in days, months, or years). How long was this period?   _____

Has this behavior ever resulted in hospitalization or injury severe enough to require medical treatment?   ❏ Yes   ❏ No

Have you ever hurt yourself with the intent to kill yourself   ❏ Yes   ❏ No

How many times have you hurt yourself on purpose throughout your life? (circle one).

One time	2–4 times	5–10 times
11–50 times	51–100 times	More than 100 times

Fig. 4.3   (continued) Note. From Heath and Nixon (2009). Copyright © 2009 by Taylor & Francis Group. Reprinted with permission

appropriate for the initial screening of NSSI. This short self-report questionnaire not only evaluates NSSI but also examines suicide-related behaviors. The SHBQ combines the ease and cost effectiveness of a self-report measure along with the rich detail provided by a clinical interview (Cloutier & Humphreys, 2009).

Mental Health Screening

Finally, Heath and Nixon (2009) recommend that the initial screening of the student who self-injures include an assessment for common co-occurring mental health challenges. In addition to the series of screening questions that Heath and Nixon recommend be asked, a quick screening for externalizing, internalizing, as well as school problems can be conducted by using the *BASC-2 Behavioral and Emotional Screening System* (Kamphaus & Reynolds, 2007). Designed for use among youth ages 3–18 years, this measure includes a 30-item self-report form appropriate for use among youth in grades 3–12 (it also includes parent and teacher forms). Psychometrically, this measure has been suggested to be a well-developed, reliable, and valid screening tool of behavioral and emotional problems (Furlong, O'Brennan, & Johnson, in press; Johnson, in press).

Concluding Comments

Risk factors are historical variables that increase the likelihood of NSSI. Warning signs are the concrete manifestations of NSSI that operate in the present, and are the cues that suggest a student may currently be engaging in these behaviors. All educators need to be vigilant for risk factors and warning signs so as to be able to make the appropriate referrals for more detailed assessment and treatment. Staff development and student education are important elements in all case finding efforts, and it is hoped that the material provided in this chapter will be helpful to the school-based mental health professional who is developing such programs.

When risk factors and warning signs are identified, initial referral and screening is necessary. This screening should include a suicide risk assessment, an NSSI risk assessment, and a mental health screening. Depending upon the results of the screening (as illustrated in Fig. 4.1) the student's parents/caregivers may be contacted and immediate treatment provided (as is the case when there is risk for suicidal behavior and/or the self-injurious behavior presents a significant health/safety risk), or they may be referred for additional assessment. Information regarding the diagnostic and psychoeducational assessment of NSSI is provided in Chapters 5 and 6.

Chapter 5
Diagnostic Assessment

Determining whether an individual is engaging in NSSI, and to what degree, is the first essential step in developing effective treatment strategies. Thus, the purpose of this chapter is to discuss the diagnostic assessment of NSSI. Topics in this chapter include the roles of diagnosis and classification, a review of various classification/diagnostic models of NSSI, guidelines for differentiating NSSI from suicidal behavior, a brief discussion of some popular assessment practices that have limited utility, and finally a description of recommended assessment practices for assisting in effective diagnostic decision making. Other assessment issues, such as psychoeducational classification issues and linking assessment to intervention, will be discussed in Chapter 6. However, before examining pertinent issues in the diagnostic assessment of self-injury, it is necessary to discuss the importance of the initial response to any student possibly engaging in NSSI.

The School-Based Assessment of NSSI: The Initial Response

The school-based assessment of a youth suspected of engaging in self-injury by an appropriate mental health professional (e.g., school psychologist) is often the first contact with a professional the youth will have in the context of his or her problem. Consequently, the initial and early response to the student is critical, and sets the stage for the remainder of assessment and treatment (Walsh, 2006). In particular, skillful management of the initial response to the problem can gain the confidence of the student, comfort the student's family members in a time of understandable stress, and correctly identify the unique features of the student's self-injury. Conversely, mishandling the initial response to NSSI can have potential long-term negative repercussions. For example, a mistaken diagnosis can lead to a student's behavior being erroneously labeled as suicidal, possibly resulting in unnecessary psychiatric hospitalizations and related stigmatization (Walsh, 2006).

An appropriate and successful initial response is also important for developing a positive and therapeutic alliance with the student (Heath & Nixon, 2009; Nafisi & Stanley, 2007), particularly if the school-based mental health professional conducting the assessment is also involved in the student's treatment. Unfortunately,

D.N. Miller, S.E. Brock, *Identifying, Assessing, and Treating Self-Injury at School*,
Developmental Psychopathology at School, DOI 10.1007/978-1-4419-6092-4_5,
© Springer Science+Business Media, LLC 2010

developing a positive alliance with students exhibiting NSSI is often difficult to accomplish. For example, students who engage in NSSI are frequently concerned about how their self-injury will be perceived by others (Heath & Nixon, 2009). Additionally, research indicates that even experienced mental health and medical professionals find self-injuring behavior to be among the most difficult and upsetting behaviors they encounter in their work (Connors, 2000; Dieter, Nicholls, & Pearlman, 2000).

Professionals who work with individuals engaging in self-injury often report being perplexed and disturbed by the behavior, and regard it with disgust and a sense of helplessness (D'Onofrio, 2007; Walsh, 2006). It is therefore critical that mental health professionals in the schools increase their knowledge about NSSI so that they can respond to students engaging in it in a more confident, empathetic, and compassionate manner. As noted by D'Onofrio (2007), "The effective helper understands that the starting point for engagement is making contact with the individual *behind* the behavior and recognizing the suffering that underscores the injurer's self-destructive acts" (p. 118).

There are several issues school-based mental health professionals should keep in mind when first encountering a student who is either suspected of or currently engaging in NSSI. First, it is essential that school personnel neither *underreact* nor *overreact* to NSSI. Not reacting with sufficient urgency to NSSI is problematic for many reasons, including ethical ones, and sends the message to youth that their problems are not being treated seriously. This message, although unintended, will likely undermine any trust or alliance between the student and the professional. An overreaction to NSSI, often characterized by shock, revulsion, or excessive concern, can negatively affect the relationship and alliance between the professional and the student as well. What is most likely to be effective is to provide a calm, dispassionate, low-key response when first encountering the issue of NSSI with a student (Walsh, 2006), focusing on listening to the student's perspectives on his or her problems and emotional well-being (Heath & Nixon, 2009). Effective listening skills are critical in the school-based assessment of NSSI. Indeed, Walsh (2006) states that "the secret to understanding and treating self-injury is first and foremost developing an ability to really listen" (p. xiv).

Although of critical importance, effective listing skills are necessary but not sufficient for increasing the probability of effective school-based assessment and treatment of NSSI. For this to occur, school personnel must not only listen, but also provide an appropriate initial response to a student when confronted by the presence of self-injury. For example, when first assessing and responding to self-injury, D'Onofrio (2007) suggests that what is often the first and perhaps the most problematic response to a self-injurer is to try to make the student stop the behavior. Efforts designed to cajole or convince students to stop engaging in self-injury are not only usually ineffective, they also frequently backfire. Although attempting to convince students to stop engaging in self-injury may be a natural and understandable response, such a response is often interpreted by students as not being helpful or considerate, and often results in a power struggle that may seriously erode trust. As noted by D'Onofrio (2007), "When the helper imposes his or her desire for the client to get better, the ensuing power struggle creates an impasse in the relationship that ultimately diminishes the helper's leverage in helping the client" (p. 113).

The Issue of "Contracts"

A common mistake that some professionals make when they first encounter an individual engaging in NSSI is to make what is essentially a "contract" with the student not to engage in self-injurious behaviors. This practice is problematic because "asking clients to give up self-injury when it is their best emotion-regulation technique can be both unrealistic and invalidating" (Walsh, 2007, p. 1061). Students may view such "contracts" as an implicit form of condemnation, which will have deleterious effects on the relationship between the student and the school-based mental health professional. Walsh (2007) recommends that a more effective strategy would be to emphasize that the student learn new skills for emotional regulation rather than "forbidding" NSSI.

The issue of "safety contracts" also applies to individuals exhibiting suicidal behavior, and briefly mentioning the use of contracts in this context may be instructive. Similar to safety contracts for NSSI, "safety" or "no-suicide" contracts are verbal or written agreements that are negotiated with suicidal individuals in the hope that it will improve intervention compliance and decrease the probability of further suicidal behavior (Miller & Eckert, 2009). Although such "no-suicide" contracts have been used quite frequently, particularly in outpatient settings (Berman, Jobes, & Silverman, 2006), their use has been criticized because of the perception that it provides mental health professionals with a false sense of security and decreased clinical vigilance (Goin, 2003). For example, Jobes (2003) has suggested that "safety contracts are neither contractual nor do they ensure genuine safety, because they tend to emphasize what patients *won't* do versus what they *will* do" (p. 3). A recent literature review examining the utility of such contracts with suicidal individuals found no empirical support for them, leading the authors to propose the use of *commitment to treatment statements* as an alternative (Rudd, Mandrusiak, & Joiner, 2006). School-based mental health professionals are therefore encouraged to adopt similar practices when working with students engaging in NSSI.

Suggestions and Guidelines When First Responding to NSSI

Walsh (2006) provides several other helpful and practical suggestions when first responding to youth who may be engaging in self-injury, including (a) avoiding the use of suicide terminology; (b) using the student's own descriptive language strategically; (c) gently challenging language that is minimizing or too idiosyncratic; (d) conveying respectful curiosity; and (e) being nonjudgmental and compassionate at all times.

Avoid the Use of Suicide Terminology

A common mistake is the failure among some mental health and medical professionals to adequately distinguish between self-injury and suicidal behavior. When
assessing a student, it is critical to be able to determine the intent of the self-injury,
so that a determination can be made as to whether or not the student is suicidal.
Assuming that it has been determined that the student's self-injurious behaviors
do not have a suicidal intent, professionals in schools should avoid referring to
the student as making a "suicide gesture." Not only is that description in this case
inaccurate, it also implies that a behavior is "not a real suicide attempt" and therefore undeserving of serious alarm or concern. Moreover, the term "suicide gesture"
implies that the behavior may be manipulative. Self-injury is neither insignificant
nor manipulative (Walsh, 2006).

Use the Student's Own Descriptive Language Strategically

Walsh (2006) suggests that, except under certain circumstances, it is often quite
helpful to employ the language of self-injurers themselves when communicating
with them. Most individuals who engage in NSSI use descriptive language when
they speak or write of their self-injury, such as "cutting," "carving," "scratching,"
"burning," and "hitting." There are a number of advantages of using such language
with students engaging in NSSI. For example, using the student's own language is
a useful "joining" strategy, and is also respectful of and empowering to the student.
A second advantage of "mirroring" a student's language is that it is a preliminary
step in entering what Walsh (2006) refers to as the "psychological space" (p. 73)
of the individual engaging in NSSI, which is crucial for understanding the person,
exhibiting empathy for him or her, and promoting a therapeutic alliance.

Gently Challenge Minimizing or Idiosyncratic Language

Although using a student's own language is often a useful strategy in the assessment
and intervention process, there are situations in which this is not the case and using
the student's own language is ill-advised. For example, if a student is performing
considerable self-harm to his or her body but the student's language does not reflect
the degree of damage inflicted – a process Walsh (2006) refers to as "minimization"
(p. 73) – the student's actual choice of language should *not* be mirrored (e.g., if a
student is engaging in severe and repetitive cutting behaviors, but describing their
behavior as "scratching," the mental health professional working with the student
would not want to mirror this inaccurate descriptor). A second example of a situation
in which mirroring the student's own language would not be recommended involves
students referring to their behavior in an ultrasubjective or idiosyncratic manner; a
situation that most typically occurs when an individual is exhibiting some form of
psychosis, such as schizophrenia (Walsh, 2006).

Convey Respect and Curiosity

Kettlewell (1999), the author of a compelling memoir detailing her own past experiences with NSSI, suggested that a helpful way to initially respond to it was to do so in a manner characterized by "respectful curiosity." That is, the "tone" of the initial response that is made in the assessment context should be one in which the assessor exhibits and communicates respect for the student and an attitude of wanting to know more about the problem rather than wanting it to go away quickly (Walsh, 2006). Of course, the manner in which curiosity is conveyed should be appropriate; interest in the student that comes across as prurient or thrill seeking may be perceived as aversive or reinforcing for those engaging in NSSI. Although when assessing a particular individual, a tone of respectful curiosity is both warranted and recommended, this approach should be tempered when working with peer groups where contagion is or may be developing (Walsh, 2006).

Be Nonjudgmental and Compassionate

Exhibiting nonjudgmental compassion to students who self-injure is important, as these individuals frequently encounter criticism and pejorative reactions and judgments from others for their behavior. Responding in a calm, nonjudgmental, and compassionate manner to a student who engages in NSSI can be an immensely relieving experience for that individual (Walsh, 2006). Doing so will likely enhance the therapeutic alliance, and increase the probability that the student will more fully disclose their issues and concerns. Walsh (2006) also makes an interesting distinction between *compassion* (which is recommended) and *concern* and *support* (which is not). The distinctions between the two are subtle, but important. According to Walsh (2006): "Concern and support suggest a certain amount of affective intensity, a yearning to be of assistance, and a desire to quickly protect and intervene. Compassion is more about acceptance, about being with the client in a neutral, nonjudgmental way with no immediate expectations for change" (p. 78).

The initial response to a student engaging in NSSI is a critical variable in determining if the assessment of the student is likely to proceed in a productive fashion that eventually results in the student receiving effective treatment. If this response is handled skillfully and respectfully by school personnel, it increases the probability that the student will be cooperative during the assessment and respond to questions in an open, non-defensive, and accurate manner.

Physical Assessment of Self-Injury

A physical assessment should be part of the initial evaluation of students engaging in self-injury. In schools, this assessment would be most appropriately conducted by the school nurse (Shapiro, 2008) or some other appropriately credentialed medical professional. This professional can and should play an important role in the school-based assessment and treatment of NSSI (McDonald, 2006) and should be a member on any school's crisis intervention team (a topic discussed in Chapter 7). Clearly, if wounds resulting from self-injury require immediate first aid, they should be dressed and bandaged by the school nurse or some other medical professional prior to any further assessment (Shapiro, 2008).

Diagnostic Assessment: Assets and Limitations

When conducting a diagnostic assessment of NSSI, it is necessary to understand the advantages of diagnostic assessment in general, as well as its limitations. Although the fields of psychology and education have been grappling with the sometimes controversial issue of diagnosis and classification for decades, practitioners, researchers, policy makers, and others generally agree about the importance of diagnostic assessment for a variety of reasons. These include (a) enhancing communication among professionals and others; (b) providing the ability to more easily communicate and share information, thereby ensuring more efficient delivery of services; (c) determining needs for services; (d) facilitating research and practice; and (e) providing a mechanism for financial reimbursement of services (Dowdy, Mays, Kamphaus, & Reynolds, 2009).

Diagnostic assessment also has some clear limitations as well. For example, a primary concern with current diagnostic systems is the over-reliance on the use of purely categorical methods (Dowdy et al., 2009). Categorical systems, such as the *DSM-IV-TR* and the *IDEIA*, use specific decision rules to determine membership in a specific category. These systems are dichotomous; one either has or does not have membership in the diagnostic category. That is, a child is classified as either having a disability (*IDEIA*) or a mental disorder (*DSM-IV-TR*) or not. However, many disorders or disabilities are more accurately conceptualized as existing on a continuum (Dowdy et al., 2009). For example, one adolescent could be mildly depressed, a second adolescent could be moderately depressed, and a third could be severely depressed. In each case the diagnostic category (depression) is the same. However, the *degree* of depression for each of these hypothetical individuals is markedly different, and could (and often will) lead to different forms of intervention.

Moreover, there appears to be a lack of "goodness of fit" between current categorical diagnostic systems and "clinical reality" (Jablensky, 1999). Specifically, evidence suggests that there are no true or clinically meaningful qualitative points where individuals should be "diagnosed" or separated (Sroufe, 1997). Indeed, throughout the scientific literature there is ample evidence suggesting that symptoms of child and adolescent disorders such as hyperactivity/impulsivity, inattention, conduct problems, depression, and anxiety occur along a continuum (Dowdy et al., 2009).

A major problem with categorical diagnostic systems is their potential to overlook children and adolescents with significant problems but who do not meet diagnostic criteria for a particular mental disorder or educational disability (Dowdy et al., 2009). Additionally, many children who are classified by school person-nel as having a disability often receive services only after they exhibit significant problems or impairment. This "wait-to-fail" approach often provides services much later than they are needed. If services were implemented earlier, when children are exhibiting sub-syndromal psychopathology or high risk status for the development of psychopathology, they would have a much higher probability of being effective.

As a result of the dissatisfaction with categorical systems of classification, dimen-sional models of classification have been proposed. Unlike categorical models, which assume that behavior occurs dichotomously, dimensional models concep-tualize behavior along a continuum (Dowdy et al., 2009). A major advantage of such an approach is that grouping behaviors by constructs (or dimensions) allows for the classification of all children and adolescents on a particular dimension or even several dimensions of behavior (Meehl, 1995). There are other advantages to using a dimensional approach to classification as well. For example, dimen-sional approaches can have greater predictive validity than categorical methods (Fergusson & Horwood, 1995), they measure comorbidity more precisely (Caron & Rutter, 1991), and they represent categorical disorders like personality disorder with greater accuracy (Garb, 1996). Using a dimensional approach allows practitioners to classify the full range of behavior for all children evaluated, much in the same way that the variables of height and weight are measured.

Because both categorical approaches and dimensional approaches to diagnostic assessment have particular strengths, it has been recommended that practitioners merge these two assessment approaches as much as possible (Kamphaus & Frick, 1996). However, most diagnostic systems for mental disorders, such as the *DSM*, are categorical in nature. Two categorical diagnostic systems that have been proposed to classify different types of self-injury, and the potential utility of these systems for school practitioners, are described below.

Favazza's Diagnostic System

As noted in Chapter 1, NSSI is not currently listed as a separate psychiatric dis-order in the *DSM-IV-TR* (American Psychiatric Association [APA], 2000). In the DSM, the behaviors associated with NSSI historically have been commonly viewed as symptoms within the context of other disorders, such as borderline personality disorder (D'Onofrio, 2007; Favazza, 1998). It has been suggested that the limited research on NSSI and its relatively recent emergence as a serious psychological problem has delayed its potential categorization as a distinct nosological entity (Simeon & Favazza, 2001).

Favazza (1996) proposed that NSSI should be included as a new Axis I diag-nostic category in the *DSM* under the name Repetitive Self-Mutilation Syndrome (RSM), which he defined as a "recurrent failure to resist impulses to harm one's body physically without suicidal intent" (p. 253). However, because this cate-gory does not exist in the current version of the *DSM*, Favazza has recommended that clinicians consider the diagnosis of Impulse Control Disorder, Not Otherwise Specified for individuals engaging in this kind of NSSI. Currently, the only mention of self-injurious behavior as described in the *DSM* (other than in the context of developmental disabilities) is in the diagnostic criteria for Borderline Personality Disorder (BPD). To meet diagnostic criteria for BPD, an individual would have to exhibit five or more out of a possible nine behaviors, one of which could be "recurrent suicidal behavior, gestures, or threats, or self-mutilating behavior" (*DSM-IV-TR*, APA, 2000 p. 710). Consequently, school personnel looking to the *DSM* for guidance in diagnostic classification and decision making will not find it to be particularly helpful.

In addition to the *DSM*, a number of other diagnostic classification systems for NSSI have been proposed, including those developed by Menninger (1966), Ross and McKay (1979), and Walsh and Rosen (1988). A diagnostic system that in recent years has become influential was developed over time by Favazza and colleagues (Favazza, 1987; Favazza, 1996; Favazza, 1998; Favazza & Ronsenthal, 1990; Simeon & Favazza, 2001) and has widely been considered an important advance in the diagnostic assessment of self-injury (Walsh, 2006). Simeon and Favazza (2001) propose that self-injurious behavior be organized into four major categories: (a) stereotypic, (b) major, (c) compulsive, and (d) impulsive. Each of these categories is described briefly below, with a particular emphasis on impulsive self-injury, as this category is the most pertinent for readers of this text.

Stereotypic Self-Injury

This category refers to "highly repetitive, monotonous, fixed, often rhythmic, seemingly highly driven, and usually contentless (i.e., devoid of thought, affect, and meaning) acts, which can widely range in self-inflicted tissue injury from mild to severe or even life-threatening at times" (Simeon & Favazza, 2001, p. 6). In contrast to other categories, individuals exhibiting stereotypic self-injury are less likely to display NSSI in private, are commonly associated with some degree of mental retardation, and appear more strongly driven by biology. Common conditions associated with stereotypic self-injury include autism and other developmental disabilities and medical diseases/disorders such as Lesch–Nyhan, Cornelia de Lange, and Prader–Willi (Simeon & Favazza, 2001).

Major Self-Injury

This category "encompasses the most dramatic and often life-threatening forms of self-injury and involves major and often irreversible destruction to body tissue" (Simeon & Favazza, 2001, p. 8). Castration, eye enucleation, and (to a lesser degree) amputation of extremities are the most common forms of major self-injury, which often occur as isolated rather than repetitive behaviors. Individuals exhibiting major self-injury are likely to be psychotic, with schizophrenia being the most frequent disorder. When exhibited by psychotic individuals, major self-injury typically occurs within the context of delusions and/or hallucinations, the most prominent of which are frequently associated with sexual temptation, sin, self-punishment, and salvation (Simeon & Favazza, 2001).

Compulsive Self-Injury

This category includes "repetitive, often ritualistic behaviors that typically occur multiple times per day, such as trichotillomania (hair pulling), onychophagia (nail biting), and skin picking or skin scratching (neurotic excoriations)" (Simeon & Favazza, 2001, p. 9). Of these, trichotillomania has by far received the most investigation from researchers. Individuals who engage in compulsive self-injury often describe increased anxiety followed by subsequent tension relief after engaging in NSSI (Simeon & Favazza, 2001).

Impulsive Self-Injury

This category includes those behaviors that "can be conceptualized as acts of impulsive aggression [and] frequently permit those who engage in them to obtain rapid but short-lived relief from various intolerable states" (Simeon & Favazza, 2001, p. 15). The most common behaviors in this category "include skin cutting, skin burning, self sticking with pins, and various ways of self-hitting using one's own body parts, objects, or by throwing oneself against objects" (Simeon & Favazza, 2001, p. 15). According to Simeon and Favazza (2001), individuals who can be classified in this category exhibit

- a preoccupation with harming themselves physically
- recurrent failure to resist impulses to harm themselves physically, resulting in the destruction or alteration of body tissue
- an increasing sense of tension immediately prior to the act of self-injury
- a sense of relief or gratification when committing self-injury
- no conscious suicidal intent, and the behavior is not a result of psychosis, transexualism, mental retardation, or developmental disabilities

Favazza (1996) has proposed using the terms *episodic* and *repetitive* as two subtypes within this diagnostic category. In the episodic type, self-injury will occur irregularly and may be exhibited only a limited number of times. Although these individuals harm themselves for psychological purposes (e.g., to feel better; to regain a sense of control), they typically do not self-identify as "cutters" or "burners." However, in the repetitive type self-injury may have an addictive quality and become a predominant preoccupation, eventually becoming incorporated into the individual's sense of identity, and may become an almost automatic response to various disturbing internal and external stimuli (Simeon & Favazza, 2001). As such, the episodic subcategory includes the same types of behaviors (cutting, burning, and picking) as the repetitive, but the individual is not as preoccupied with engaging in self-injury, and engages in it less frequently (Walsh, 2006).

Although the attempt at providing more precision to the classification of NSSI by Favazza and colleagues is widely considered to be a considerable improvement over previous classification models, it is not without its problems. For example, as Simeon and Favazza (2001) acknowledge, the distinction between compulsive self-injury and impulsive-repetitive self-injury is not always clear. Additionally, individuals who engage in NSSI are frequently quite fluid in how they harm themselves, and may exhibit both compulsive and impulsive self-injury at the same time. For example, Walsh (2006) reported working with a female client who exhibited compulsive (hair pulling), impulsive-repetitive (frequent cutting), and impulsive-episodic (occasional methodical cutting) forms of NSSI simultaneously. Such convergence of diverse behaviors within single individuals suggests that the associations between the impulsive and compulsive categories may not be very strong (Walsh, 2006).

What appears to be a simpler and more practical classification scheme of NSSI has recently been developed by Walsh (2006), building on previous work done by Farberow (1980), and Pattison and Kahan (1983). This classification system, which categorizes self-injury as either direct or indirect self-harm, appears to be highly useful for practicing clinicians, including school personnel, and can be more directly linked to treatment.

Walsh's Classification Scheme for Direct and Indirect Self-Harm

Walsh's (2006) classification scheme makes use of the concepts of direct and indirect self-harm, combined with the dimensions of lethality and the number of episodes/occurrences of the behavior. Although the form of self-injury as described in this text clearly fits under the "direct self-harm" category in Walsh's classification scheme, it is important for school personnel to assess the presence and frequency of indirect self-harm behaviors as well, as these can have important implications for treatment.

Direct Self-Harm

Direct self-harm "refers to behavior that involves immediate tissue damage and for which intent is generally unambiguous" (Walsh, 2006, p. 22). This category applies to individuals who deliberately hurt themselves, causing immediate damage. The main types of direct self-harm include suicidal behavior, major self-injury (e.g., self-enucleation), and common forms of self-injury (e.g., cutting, burning). These types can range from high-lethality behaviors (e.g., suicide) to medium-lethality (e.g., recurrent suicide attempts, major self-injury) to low-lethality (e.g., self-injury) behaviors. Moreover, the behaviors can involve either single or multiple episodes (Walsh, 2006).

Indirect Self-Harm

Indirect self-harm "refers to behavior in which the damage is generally accumulative (and/or deferred) rather than immediate" (Walsh, 2006, p. 23), and intent is often ambiguous. Common examples of indirect self-harm include the unauthorized discontinuance or abuse of prescribed medications, and patterns of substance abuse and eating disorders that damage physical health. For both substance abuse and eating disorders, physical harm is usually accumulative rather than immediate, although acute alcohol poisoning or drug overdoses are clear exceptions. Additionally, individuals who abuse substances or who have eating disorders tend to deny self-destructive intent (Walsh, 2006).

Another type of indirect self-harm is risk taking. Walsh (2006) describes three types of risk taking, including (a) situational, (b) physical, and (c) sexual. Situational risk taking refers to behaviors that are not risky in and of themselves, but may be potentially harmful in certain contexts (Walsh, 2006). For example, taking a walk is not typically a dangerous activity, but it can become one if done late at night in a high-crime area. Some individuals may be more likely to put themselves in dangerous situations due to poor judgment and/or a minimal concern or investment in living (Walsh, 2006). According to Walsh, an assessment of an individual's level of situational risk taking can be accomplished by asking the following questions:

- "Do you ever walk in a dangerous area of a city alone at night?"
- "Have you ever gotten into a car with strangers?"
- "Do you ever hitchhike alone?"
- "Do you place yourself in risky situations?" (p. 26)

Physical risk taking is a second type of risk-taking behavior, and many engaging in NSSI tend to be physical risk-takers (Lightfoot, 1997; Ponton, 1997). Examples of physical risk taking may include walking in high-speed traffic, sitting on the edge of a roof of a multistory building, and straddling an open stairway at a high elevation (Walsh, 2006). Many adolescents report feelings of exhilaration when they take physical risks (Ponton, 1997), even though a slight miscalculation in such instances can lead to serious injury or even death (Walsh, 2006). According to Walsh, an assessment of an individual's degree of physical risk taking can be accomplished by asking the following questions:

- "Do you ever take physical risks, such as walking in high-speed traffic or standing on the edge of a roof?"
- "Have you done risky things, such as walk on train tracks in a tunnel?"
- "Do you find physically risky activities thrilling?" (p. 26)

A third form of physical risk taking is sexual risk-taking behavior, which comes in many forms. Examples of this type of behavior include having unprotected sex with strangers, having multiple sexual partners within a short period of time, engaging in sex with intravenous drug users or with individuals known to have sexually transmitted diseases, and having sex while intoxicated and being unaware of one's activities (Walsh, 2006). Such behaviors, especially when done with great frequency, are potentially highly self-destructive, even if such behavior may not be consciously intended. According to Walsh, an assessment of an individual's sexual risk taking can be accomplished by asking the following questions:

- "Have you ever had sex with people you barely know?"
- "Have you had sex while intoxicated and had little or no memory of the experience afterward?"
- "Have you ever had unprotected sex?"
- "How many sexual partners have you had in the last year?"
- "Do you think of your sexual behavior as risky?" (p. 26)

Walsh (2006) advises that the series of questions listed above should be done with considerable care and compassion. Forming a therapeutic alliance with the youth engaging in NSSI (a subject for the next chapter) typically has to be well established before useful and reliable information can be obtained, especially about issues regarding sexual behavior. As noted by Walsh (2006):

> Inquiring about these risk-taking behaviors should be done in a supportive, nonjudgmental manner. Clients should not feel that they are being subjected to an evaluation of their morality. The goal is to assess the person's self-destructiveness in all its manifestations. The presence of these major forms of indirect self-harm points to the client being in significant distress and lacking important coping skills. Both should be targeted in treatment. (p. 27)

School personnel may make use of the classification system developed by Walsh (2006), and are referred to his text for a more detailed discussion. This classification system can provide a useful starting point for diagnostic assessment, while also providing needed information for an individual's level of other self-destructive behaviors, as the presence of one or more of these behaviors will have important implications for treatment. In particular, given that youth engaging in self-injury are often erroneously described as engaging in suicidal behavior, as well as the high degree of comorbidity between these two problems, it is critical that mental health professionals in the schools have the knowledge and skills in diagnostic assessment to accurately distinguish between them.

Differentiating Self-Injury from Suicidal Behavior

Although there is a high degree of overlap between NSSI and suicidal behavior (as discussed in Chapters 3 and 4), and the relationship between them is complex, these two problem behaviors should be understood and treated differently (Walsh, 2006).

Useful and practical guidelines containing nine points of distinction for determining whether a self-destructive behavior is suicidal or self-injurious is provided by Walsh and summarized below.

Intent

Walsh (2006) suggests that assessing the individual's intent is a fundamental place to begin in differentiating youth suicidal behavior from NSSI. Essentially, when considering intent, the school practitioner needs to assess what the individual intends to accomplish by engaging in the self-destructive behavior. In other words, what is the goal of the behavior? For example, if during interview an adolescent girl is asked why she cuts herself and responds, "I cut myself to feel better" and denied any suicidal intent, this would suggest the student does engage in NSSI, but is not currently suicidal. In contrast, a statement such as "No one cares about me and no one ever will – life just isn't worth living anymore" clearly suggests a greater possibility of suicidality. Unfortunately, mental health professionals often find it difficult to elicit a clear articulation of intent from the individuals they are assessing. Youth who engage in self-destructive behavior are frequently emotionally overwhelmed, as well as very confused about their own behavior (Walsh, 2006), and as a result often provide answers to the question of intent that are ambiguous (e.g., "It seemed like the right thing to do at the time") or simply not very helpful (e.g., "I don't know").

Assessing intent can be a relatively simple matter, but it is frequently complex and requires a combination of compassion and investigative persistence (Walsh, 2006). Both individuals who are suicidal and individuals who engage in NSSI typically experience a tremendous amount of psychological pain. The suicidal individual will do whatever it takes to make this pain, which the eminent suicidologist Edwin S. Shneidman referred to as *psychache*, go away *permanently* (Shneidman, 1996). In contrast, "the intent of the self-injuring person is not to *terminate* consciousness, but to *modify* it" (Walsh, 2006, p. 7). That is, in most instances youth who engage in NSSI do so not to die, but rather to relieve painful emotions. In most cases, these individuals appear to hurting themselves to relieve the presence of too *much* emotion, such as anger, shame, sadness, frustration, contempt, anxiety, tension, or panic. Others, who appear to be in the minority, appear to hurt themselves to relieve too *little* emotion or states of dissociation (Walsh, 2006).

Level of Physical Damage and Potential Lethality

The chosen method of self-harm by an individual often communicates a great deal about the intent of the behavior. For example, the use of firearms is the most frequently used method among adolescents who die by suicide, followed by hanging (Berman et al., 2006). Both of these methods are highly lethal, and in general, the stronger the intention an individual has to commit suicide, the greater the potential lethality of the method selected to carry out that intention (Miller & Eckert, 2009). In contrast, research conducted with 469 adolescent suicide *attempters* found that the two most common methods were drug ingestion overdose and wrist cutting, respectively (Reynolds & Mazza, 1993). This suggests that youth who attempt suicide should not be viewed synonymously with youth who commit suicide; there are often important distinctions between them, including the potential lethality and level of physical damage of their chosen methods (Miller & Eckert, 2009).

The most common form of self-harm among youth who engage in NSSI is skin cutting. However, among youth who die by suicide, only a very small percentage (less than 1%) die as result of cutting themselves. Consequently, when assessing whether a student intends suicide or NSSI, the method or methods these students use to engage in self-destructive behavior will provide critical information. It should be noted that the type of cutting that is most likely to result in death is severing the carotid artery or jugular veins in the neck. It is not the cutting of the arms or legs, the most common bodily locations for those who engage in NSSI (Walsh, 2006).

Frequency of the Behavior

In general, NSSI occurs at much higher rates than suicide attempts. Most youth who attempt suicide do so infrequently, whereas youth who engage in NSSI often do so at a high rate. Although there are a small percentage of youth who attempt suicide on a fairly regular basis, these individuals most often appear to ingest pills (a low-lethality method) and frequently disclose their suicide attempts to others, typically resulting in preventative measures being undertaken. However, even compared to youth who engage in recurrent suicide attempts, many if not most youth who engage in NSSI do so at a much higher rate.

Multiple Methods

More research is needed in this area, but there are some indications that, in comparison with youth who make suicide attempts, youth who engage in NSSI are more likely to use multiple methods (Walsh, 2006). The reasons for this are unclear, although they may be related to issues related to preference and circumstances. For example, many youth engaging in NSSI report their preference for using multiple methods. However, adolescents who are placed in more restricted settings, such as a hospital or group home, may have greater difficulty accessing particular devices (e.g., razors) for cutting themselves, and may then have to use other methods of self-injury (e.g., hitting themselves) to achieve desired effects (Walsh, 2006).

Level of Psychological Pain

Suicidal individuals do not want to die as much as they want their psychological pain and suffering to end (Shneidman, 1996). However, because their attempts at reducing their pain have not been successful, they may view death as the only viable option for accomplishing this goal (Miller & Eckert, 2009). Consequently, suicide is often viewed by youth as their only means of escape from a level of psychological pain they may view as unendurable. In contrast, although the emotional pain of an individual engaging in NSSI is intense and often extremely uncomfortable, it typically does not reach the level of a suicidal crisis (Walsh, 2006).

Constriction of Cognition

Shneidman (1985, 1996) has often pointed out that suicidal people frequently exhibit cognitive constrictions or "tunnel vision," in which they engage in dichoto-mous, "either–or" modes of thinking. For example, a suicidal individual may think "if my girlfriend dumps me, I can't bear to live." The suicidal individual often engages in an "all-or-nothing" style of thinking, and these cognitive distortions can have deadly consequences. In contrast, individuals who engage in NSSI are characterized less by constrictive thinking than by disorganized thinking (Walsh, 2006). Unlike many people who are suicidal, people who engage in NSSI do not see their choices as limited; they simply make bad choices (e.g., cutting themselves to reduce emotional stress rather than to deal with this problem in a more appropriate, constructive, and socially acceptable manner).

Helplessness and Hopelessness

Both helplessness (Seligman, 1992) and hopelessness (Beck, Rush, Shaw, & Emery, 1979) have long been associated with suicidal behavior. In contrast, individuals who engage in NSSI frequently do not exhibit these particular cognitive distortions (Walsh, 2006). Unlike people who are suicidal, who often perceive themselves as having no control over their psychological pain, for many individuals the option of self-injury provides a needed sense of control. In fact, many students engaging in NSSI may find it to be reassuring that cutting, burning, or some other form of self-harm is most likely quickly available when needed.

Psychological Aftermath of the Self-Harm Incident

For the individual who engages in NSSI, the aftermath of the self-harm is often quite positive, as in many cases the function of the behavior is to relieve emotional distress. Moreover, not only is the self-harm effective in relieving distressful emotions, it frequently does so immediately. In contrast, most individuals who survive suicide often report feeling no better after their attempt, and may feel worse (Walsh, 2006). When a student engaging in NSSI reports it is no longer effective for achieving desired outcomes such as reduced tension, the school-based mental health professional should monitor the situation carefully, as the probability of suicidal behavior may increase.

A Final Note of Caution

Although the variables described above can be used to differentiate and distinguish students engaging in NSSI from those who are engaging in more serious forms of self-destructive behavior (e.g., suicide attempts), school personnel should be sufficiently aware that engaging in NSSI is a serious risk factor for later suicidal behavior. As noted by Joiner (2009) in his influential and increasingly empirically supported interpersonal-psychological theory of suicidal behavior, people essentially die by suicide "because they can, and because they want to" (p. 244). For individuals to die by suicide, they first have to want to die by suicide – a process Joiner believes occurs because of severe psychological pain that results from a combination of perceived burdensomeness and failed belongingness (Joiner, 2005, 2009).

The desire for death, however, is considered by Joiner to be necessary but not sufficient for suicide to occur. The individual must also be *capable* of committing suicide, a behavior that is exceedingly difficult to do given that human beings are genetically wired for self-preservation. For Joiner, the only ones who are capable of death by suicide are those individuals who become habituated to it through sufficient experiences of pain and provocation, especially involving intentional self-injury. When the ability to commit suicide is present, as well as the desire for death, the probability of suicide greatly increases (Joiner, 2005, 2009). Consequently, even students who engage in NSSI and are deemed not to be suicidal should be carefully monitored, as their self-injurious behaviors place them at much higher risk for suicide than students who do not engage in NSSI.

Making the distinction of whether a student's self-destructive behavior is suicidal or not is critical. To do this most effectively, it is necessary to understand which assessment methods will most likely provide reliable and valid answers to this question, as well as other important questions that will arise in the assessment process. Some assessment methods are more useful than others in the assessment of NSSI, and these are discussed in greater detail below. First, however, a brief overview of the assessment process is provided.

Assessment Methods, Sources, and Settings

Merrell (2008a, 2008b) has provided a model for conducting school-based social/emotional/behavioral assessments that can be applied to a variety of problems, including NSSI. In this assessment model, multiple methods of assessment (e.g., self-report measures, rating scales, interviews, direct observations) are used across multiple informants (e.g., students, teachers, parents/caregivers) and settings (e.g., school, home; community). A brief overview of some pertinent issues to be considered in terms of assessment methods, sources, and settings is provided next, followed by a more extensive discussion of particular assessment methods and practices.

Assessment Methods

Because each particular method, instrument, or source used in the collection of assessment data is subject to error, an aggregated, comprehensive approach can be useful for overcoming the limitations of any particular assessment component (Merrell, 2008b). Methods in the assessment of child and adolescent psychological disorders, including NSSI, may potentially include direct observations, record reviews, behavior rating scales, interviews, self-report measures, and projective techniques (Merrell, 2008b).

Assessment Sources

The many potential sources of assessment information include the particular student who is being evaluated, his or her parents or caregivers, other family members, teachers and other school personnel, the student's friends and peers, and possibly community-based informants such as youth group leaders or other service providers (Merrell, 2008b). Some of these sources, however, will be more valuable than others in assessing NSSI. In particular, the most important individuals to assess typically are the student, his or her parents or caregivers, and his or her teachers. Because NSSI is an internalizing problem involving internal perceptions and states, and because other adults in the student's environment are often not aware of their self-injurious behavior, the student suspected of engaging in NSSI is widely considered to be the primary assessment source, and obtaining the student's self-report (through both interviews and self-report scales) is widely considered to be the most critical assessment method. Possible exceptions to this general rule include the assessment of very young children, youth who are unwilling to provide information about themselves, or students with limited cognitive and/or verbal skills. In these situations, parents, caregivers, and school personnel may provide the most useful information (Merrell, 2008b).

Assessment Settings

Assessment settings refer to the particular places in which assessment information is based rather than the actual settings in which data are collected or where meetings occur. For example, although parents or caregivers may meet with the school psychologist in his or her office to provide information about the student's emotional problems, the setting in which the assessment is based is the student's home. Possible settings for obtaining information include school, home, various clinics or agencies, or other community settings (Merrell, 2008b).

Assessment Methods with Limited Utility

School practitioners interested in assessing students for possible emotional and/or behavioral problems, including NSSI, are presented with a variety of possible options, including the use of school record reviews, sociometric techniques, and projective techniques. However, with the possible exception of school record reviews (Brock & Clinton, 2007), in comparison with other assessment procedures these methods typically do not provide as much clinically useful information, often lack empirical support for their utility, and are not as clearly linked to problem solving (Miller, 2010). As such, these methods generally have limited utility in the assessment process, whether for diagnostic or other assessment purposes.

In particular, the use of projective techniques can be problematic. Projective techniques are assessment methods in which unstructured stimuli (e.g., inkblots, pictures) are presented to individuals who are then expected to respond verbally or motorically (e.g., drawing) depending on the requirements of the task (Miller & Nickerson, 2006). Although the popularity of these techniques has declined in recent years, they continue to be used by school-based mental health professionals (Hosp & Reschly, 2002; Shapiro & Heick, 2004; Wilson & Reschly, 1996) and to be viewed as important in the assessment process (Kennedy, Faust, Willis, & Piotrowski, 1994). For example, results from a recent national survey of school psychologists indicated that projective techniques were generally viewed as moderately useful across grade levels and for multiple purposes, including special education eligibility determination and intervention development (Hojnoski, Morrison, Brown, & Matthews, 2006).

Despite their wide use in schools, projective techniques have consistently been criticized (Dawes, 1994; Lilienfield, Wood, & Garb, 2000), and their use with children and adolescents remains controversial. Although many promote their use in schools (e.g., Bardos, 1993; Chandler, 2003; Naglieri, 1993; Yalof, Abraham, Domingos, & Socket, 2001), others have expressed significant reservations about them (e.g., Batsche & Peterson, 1983; Gittelman-Klein, 1986; Merrell, Ervin, & Gimpel, 2006; Miller, 2010; Miller & Nickerson, 2006; Motta, Little, & Tobin, 1993). Most of the controversy surrounding projective techniques has focused on their psychometric properties, particularly their questionable degree of reliability, as well as their sometimes inadequate norms (Salvia & Ysseldyke, 2001). More recently, the incremental validity (i.e., the degree to which assessment measures provide information beyond that which is already known or that cannot be gained in some other, easier way) and treatment validity (i.e., the degree to which assessment is demonstrated to contribute to a beneficial treatment outcome) of projective techniques with children and youth have been questioned as well, with both found to be lacking (Miller & Nickerson, 2006, 2007a).

These issues, as well as an increased emphasis on evidence-based assessment practices (Mash & Hunsley, 2005) and the possibility of legal sanction arising from decisions based on the results of questionable/controversial assessment instruments (Kerr & Nelson, 2002), have led to an increased call to restrict or limit the use of projective techniques with children and youth in school settings (Knoff, 2003; Merrell et al., 2006; Miller & Nickerson, 2006). Although projective techniques may have some limited uses, such as in establishing rapport with students, in general there are many significant problems associated with their use and they are therefore not recommended for the assessment of children and youth suspected of engaging in NSSI.

Recommended Assessment Methods and Practices

A variety of assessment methods and practices may be useful in the assessment of students for the presence of NSSI. For example, teacher and parent/caregiver interviews can provide valuable information regarding the perspectives of others in the student's environment. In particular, interviewing parents/caregivers can be helpful by providing (a) a broader perspective on any problems the student may be experiencing; (b) a greater understanding of the history of the student's problems, including any previous mental health problems; and (c) information regarding how parents/caregivers may be contributing to the problem, how they react to it, and any mental health issues they may have had in the past or currently experience. Interviewing teachers is also an important component of effective assessment, especially if a particular teacher refers a student. Interviewing school personnel is particularly important if the student has communicated that he or she is engaging in NSSI to school staff, and/or if particular school-based professionals have observed the student engage in NSSI.

Given that NSSI can be primarily conceptualized as an internalizing problem, the most useful methods of assessment for students who may be exhibiting it will be those that involve the student rather than significant others in the student's environment. Moreover, given the often covert nature of NSSI, and that it is frequently difficult to directly observe, the student's own perceptions and verbal descriptions of the problem become critical sources of information. Consequently, for the diagnostic assessment of NSSI two assessment methods are particularly important: student self-report measures and individual student interviews.

Self-Report Measures

Standardized self-report measures designed for use by children and adolescents have become increasingly popular, and in recent decades there have been substantial improvements in their technical adequacy (Eckert, Dunn, Gainey, & Codding, 2000). Self-report measures are not only a recommended method for assessing internalizing problems generally, they are also widely considered an essential and perhaps the most preferred assessment method (Merrell, 2008b). Because many of the behaviors and symptoms associated with NSSI are difficult if not impossible to detect through external methods of assessment (e.g., direct observations, parent/caregiver and teacher rating scales), and because a reliable and valid self-report measure provides a structured and norm-referenced method for diagnostic and evaluative purposes, these instruments are uniquely suited to and particularly useful for assessing NSSI.

The measurement of NSSI is still in its infancy, and although self-report measures designed to assess it are available, they have to date not been typically subjected to the level of research and evaluation directed to self-report measures designed to assess other, more frequently occurring internalizing problems, such as depression and anxiety. Further, some measures include indices of suicidal as well as non-suicidal self-injury. Nevertheless, many self-report measures for NSSI would appear to be useful for diagnostic assessment as well as other purposes (e.g., treatment planning, progress monitoring). Table 5.1 lists several self-report measures for the assessment of NSSI. For more information on the psychometric properties of these instruments, the reader is referred to Cloutier and Humphreys (2009).

Table 5.1 Examples of self-report measures for the assessment of NSSI in adolescents

- *Deliberate self-harm inventory* (Gratz, 2001)
- *Functional assessment of self-mutilation* (Lloyd, Kelley, & Hope, 1997)
- *Ottawa self-injury inventory* (Nixon, Cloutier, & Aggarwal, 2002)
- *Self-harm behavior questionnaire* (Gutierrez, Osman, Barrios, & Kopper, 2001)
- *Self-harm inventory* (Sansone, Wiederman, & Sansone, 1998)
- *Self-harm survey and motivations underlying self-harm questionnaire* (Laye-Gindhu & Schonert-Reichl, 2005)
- *Self-injurious thoughts and behaviors interview* (Nock et al., 2007)
- *Self-injury inventory* (Zlotnick et al., 1997)
- *Self-injury motivation scale II* (Osuch, Noll, & Putnam, 1999)
- *Self-injury questionnaire* (Alexander, 1999)
- *Suicide attempt self-injury interview* (Linehan et al., 2006)

Individual Student Interviews

Like self-report measures, interviews should be considered an essential method for assessing NSSI in youth. Probably the oldest form of assessment, interviews vary in length, structure, and the degree to which they are formal or informal (Merrell, 2008a). In contrast to the more structured nature of self-report instruments, in which individuals respond to specific, unchanging, standardized questions, interviewing often is more flexible and open-ended and provides for a variety of student responses.

Perhaps more than any other assessment technique, conducting an effective interview requires a number of highly developed clinical skills, including interpersonal skills, observational skills, and a thorough knowledge of normal and abnormal development (Merrell, 2008a). In particular, the developmental level of the student being assessed is a critically important variable to consider when conducting student interviews (McConaughy, 2005). For example, when interviewing students who are in middle-childhood (approximately children ages 6–11 years), the interviewer should make use of familiar settings and activities, provide developmentally appropriate contextual cues (e.g., pictures, examples), request language interaction with the student, and avoid abstract questions and constant eye contact (Merrell, 2008b).

School-based mental health professionals should also be cognizant of other developmental issues as well when conducting student interviews, including the student's verbal skills and what may be described as the student's emotional vocabulary (Merrell, 2008a). This last phrase refers to the student's skill level at communicating nuanced and sometimes complex emotions and reactions in the assessment context. For example, characteristics that might be described by a mature adolescent as "tension" might be described by a younger, less mature, or less verbally sophistical student as "feeling angry." Or, what might be described by an older student as "disappointment" might be described as "feeling sad" by a younger one (Merrell, 2008a).

When interviewing students for the possible presence of NSSI, it is also important to assess their developmental thought process and self-talk (Hughes & Baker, 1991). Cognitive models of internalizing problems, such as NSSI, stress the role that thinking plays in the development and maintenance of emotional distress (Miller, 2010). In particular, these models stress an individual's belief systems, irrational thoughts, and attributions regarding events and behaviors (Beck, 1976). For example, interview responses of a student exhibiting NSSI that suggest the student may be engaging in cognitive distortions (e.g., "My boyfriend dumped me *and I will never meet anyone I cared that much about ever again*; it hurt so much that I cut myself.") indicates that the use of cognitive restructuring (Friedberg & McClure, 2002) might be considered as a major component of treatment. Conducting interviews with students suspected of engaging in NSSI is perhaps the best method for assessing cognitive variables and the degree to which they may be contributing to or helping to maintain problem behaviors.

Interviews can range from being highly structured, in which each question is standardized and sequential, to being unstructured and open-ended. In the middle of these two extremes is a type of interview known as the semi-structured interview, in which the assessor does not have a list of standardized questions yet still has a specific focus or aim (McConaughy, 2005). For example, if there was concern that a particular student might be engaging in NSSI, the interviewer might ask the student specific questions related to the extent to which the student has exhibited particular behaviors consistent with NSSI. In this situation, the interviewer would be maintaining some structure in the interview, but the questions themselves may not be standardized, and the interviewer would have the flexibility to change the course of the interview based on particular student responses.

Structured interviews, which provide standardized instructions and procedures, are perhaps the most useful type of interview for diagnostic purposes. Two structured interviews, the *Suicide Attempt Self-Injury Interview* (SASII) and the *Self-Injurious Thoughts and Behavior Interview* (SITBI), may be particularly useful in the diagnostic assessment of NSSI. The *SASII* (Linehan, Comtois, Brown, Heard, & Wagner, 2006) is a structured interview designed to assess "the frequency, method, severity, context, intent, reasons, and outcomes of self-injurious behavior" (Cloutier & Humphreys, 2009, p. 131). As is implied by the name of the interview, it is designed to assess suicidal behavior as well as non-suicidal self-injury. Items on the *SASII* were developed on the basis of existing measures of suicidal behavior and on the characteristics of both suicide attempts and self-injury as described in the professional literature.

Originally developed with clinical samples of adults, the *SASII* includes a combination of open-ended, checklist, forced-choice, Likert-type, and yes/no questions. Self-report and interviewer-rated items are included, and several items have objective referents. The *SASII* contains six subscales, including suicide intent (four items), interpersonal influence (eight items), emotion relief (six items), suicide communication (two items), lethality (three items), and rescue likelihood (two items). Two additional isolated items (i.e., suicide note and impulsiveness of episode) are also included, but are not part of the subscales. Initial studies examining various aspects of the reliability and validity of the *SASII* have been promising, although more research is clearly needed (for more information on the psychometric properties of the *SASII*, the reader is referred to Cloutier & Humphreys, 2009). Although developed primarily as a research measure, it also has clear clinical utility for a variety of purposes, including diagnostic assessment and the identification of specific targets for intervention. The *SASII* may also be useful for delineating the antecedents and consequences of NSSI, and as an instrument for ongoing monitoring of treatment outcomes (Cloutier & Humphreys, 2009).

The *Self-Injurious Thoughts and Behaviors Interview* (SITBI; Nock, Holmberg, Photos, & Michel, 2007) is a 169-item structured interview that, like the *SASII*, measures both NSSI and suicidal behavior. The *SITBI* is composed of five modules that evaluate the presence, frequency, and characteristics of (a) suicidal ideation; (b) suicidal plans; (c) suicidal gestures; (d) suicidal attempts; and (e) NSSI. However, the interview is conducted only for those modules that receive a positive endorsement for the lifetime presence of that thought or behavior (Cloutier & Humphreys, 2009). The characteristics assessed by this measure include age of onset, methods, functions, severity, antecedents, pain experience, use of alcohol and drugs during self-injurious thoughts and behaviors, impulsivity, peer influences, and self-reported future probabilities of each type of self-injurious thoughts and behaviors (Nock et al., 2007). Requiring a fairly short period of time to administer (i.e., 3–15 min), the *SITBI* has exhibited adequate reliability and validity in the studies that have examined its psychometric properties, although research in this area is limited and more is needed. Although useful as an initial assessment measure of NSSI, the authors of the *SITBI* recommend that it be followed up with a more focused and detailed assessment of self-injury if and when necessary (Cloutier & Humphreys, 2009).

Finally, although the primary focus when interviewing should be on the student suspected of possibly engaging in NSSI, it is often desirable and necessary to interview the student's parents/caregivers, teachers, and other individuals in the student's environment who have frequent opportunities to observe him or her. Parents and caregivers can provide valuable information during an interview because they typically know the student better than anyone, and are usually the only ones who can provide a comprehensive developmental history of the student, as well as have knowledge regarding the student's idiosyncratic behaviors across multiple environments and time periods (Miller, 2010). Moreover, parents and caregivers may often be among the first to have observed the student's self-injurious behaviors, and can provide their perspective on where, when, and under which situations it is most likely to occur. Parents and caregivers can be especially helpful in identifying environments outside the school where their child may be engaging in NSSI. Interviewing parents/caregivers can also be useful for assessing the sense to which they may be possibly exacerbating their child's NSSI through criticism or punitive responses to it. Similarly, interviewing teachers and other school personnel can be helpful as well, particularly if they have observed the student engaging in self-injury at school or elsewhere.

Becoming a skillful and effective interviewer requires extensive training and supervised experience. For more detailed information on developmental and other aspects of interviewing students in schools, the reader is referred to Hughes and Baker (1991), McConaughy (2005), and Merrell (2008a, 2008b).

Assessing Possible Comorbid Disorders

Chapter 3 reviewed psychological disorders associated (or comorbid) with NSSI. In conducting a comprehensive assessment of self-injury, school personnel should be aware of those disorders and conditions most highly associated with NSSI, and assess for their presence as well (e.g., suicide, mood disorders, substance abuse, eating disorders, maltreatment). In general, whenever conducting school-based assessments of social, emotional, or behavioral problems, taking a "broad-band" approach to assessment is recommended, in which a number of disorders and conditions are assessed. This can help to determine if there are other problems the student may be experiencing in addition to the problem for which he/she was initially referred (i.e., self-injury). Determining whether other disorders are present or absent has important implications not only for diagnostic purposes, but also for treatment. In general, the more mental health problems or disorders a student is experiencing, the more challenging, complex, and difficult effective treatment often becomes. Two reliable and valid broad-band assessment measures widely used in schools include the *Child Behavior Checklist* (CBCL; Achenbach, 2001) and the *Behavior Assessment System for Children* (BASC-2; Reynolds & Kamphaus, 2004).

Concluding Comments

The diagnostic assessment of youth engaging in, or suspected of engaging in, NSSI is the first step in providing an effective response to the problem. However, diagnostic decision making is made more difficult by the fact that NSSI is not currently listed as a separate diagnostic category in the *DSM*. Although classification systems like those developed by Favazza (1996) and Walsh (2006) can be helpful during the initial stages of assessment for their potential value in diagnostic decision making, they do not provide particular utility in regards to treatment. Similarly, although recommended assessment practices such as student interviews and self-report measures can provide useful diagnostic information as well as serve as potential progress monitoring tools to evaluate treatment, they too have limited treatment utility. Consequently, because the ultimate goal in conducting an assessment of NSSI is to help the individual engaging in it to acquire more socially acceptable and desirable ways for dealing with emotional conflicts, a comprehensive assessment should be one that increases the likelihood of a beneficial and therapeutic outcome. In other words, assessment should be more clearly linked to intervention, which is the topic of Chapter 6.

Chapter 6
Psychoeducational Assessment

The purpose of this chapter is to discuss the psychoeducational assessment of NSSI. Because psychoeducational assessment typically occurs within school settings, this will involve considerations as to whether the nature and degree of self-injury warrants possible special education services. Consequently, this chapter begins with a discussion of psychoeducational diagnostic and classification issues as they may relate to NSSI. A particular focus of this discussion is on the handicapping condition known as Emotional Disturbance, as this category may have particular relevance for at least some students who engage in NSSI. After reviewing this issue, the primary focus of the chapter is on a problem-solving approach to assessment, in which information gained from the assessment of NSSI is linked to the development of appropriate interventions. Finally, a brief discussion of the Internet and its relationship to self-injury among students will be provided.

NSSI, Psychoeducational Classification, and Special Education Services

Students are eligible to receive special education and related services from schools only after an Individual Education Planning (IEP) team assessment (typically including a psychoeducational evaluation) has been conducted and the team concludes that the student meets one of the 13 different categories of eligibility under the *Individuals with Disabilities Education Improvement Act*, or *IDEIA* (Nickerson, Reeves, Brock, & Jimerson, 2009). However, as noted in Chapter 1, NSSI is not listed as one of the 13 categories under *IDEIA*. Moreover, although many students who engage in NSSI may not exhibit particular academic or behavior problems that would lead to a referral for special education, given that NSSI is associated with a host of other emotional and behavioral problems increases the likelihood that youth who engage in it will receive some form of special education services. To receive these services, students must be classified as having a handicapping condition under one or more of the categories within *IDEIA*, such as Learning Disabled (LD), Other Health Impaired (OHI), or Emotionally Disturbed (ED). Although several variables should be considered prior to classifying a student as needing special education

D.N. Miller, S.E. Brock, *Identifying, Assessing, and Treating Self-Injury at School*,
Developmental Psychopathology at School, DOI 10.1007/978-1-4419-6092-4_6,
© Springer Science+Business Media, LLC 2010

services (see Chapter 1), given that NSSI is primarily an emotional/behavioral prob-
lem, school personnel may view the handicapping condition known as Emotional
Disturbance to be the most appropriate classification for a student exhibiting
NSSI.

Definition of Emotional Disturbance

To help clarify the issue of whether or not a classification of ED might be appropriate for a student engaging in NSSI, it is useful to consider its definition in detail.
The major criterion in defining an emotional disturbance is "a condition whereby
a child exhibits one or more . . .characteristics over a long period of time and to a
marked degree that adversely affects educational performance. . ." (*Individuals with
Disabilities Education Improvement Act Amendments of 2004* 300.8[c][4][i]). The
phrase "a long period of time" indicates that the problem is not transient and is
often interpreted as being present for a minimum of 6 months – a timeframe consistent with several *DSM* diagnostic categories. Additionally, the phrase "a marked
degree" suggests that the behavior in question is severe and reflects a departure
from typically functioning and normative behavior. Finally, the phrase "adversely
affects educational performance" refers to the negative impact on children's academic, behavioral, social, and emotional functioning in school. Different states have
different established guidelines regarding the manner in which school functioning is
defined, and *IDEIA* (2004) does not specify any criteria for these conditions. Thus, it
is critical for school psychologists and other appropriate school personnel to address
these issues in psychoeducational reports (Hughes, Crothers, & Jimerson, 2008).
Additionally, multidisciplinary teams can accept or reject the conclusions of the
school psychologist when determining special education eligibility.

   When the conditions described above are met, a student's emotional disturbance
may be defined as follows:

- An inability to learn that cannot be explained by intellectual, sensory, or health
  factors.
- An inability to build or maintain satisfactory interpersonal relationships with
  peers and teachers.
- Inappropriate types of behavior or feelings under normal circumstances.
- A general pervasive mood of unhappiness or depression.
- A tendency to develop physical symptoms or fears associated with personal or
  school problems.
- Includes children who are schizophrenic.
- But does not include children who are socially maladjusted, unless they are also
  determined to have an emotional disturbance as determined by evaluation.

   Youth who engage in NSSI could be eligible to receive special education services
based on an emotional disturbance classification, although the definition above is

not without problems. For example, the definition is vague and subjective; what are "satisfactory" peer and teacher relationships? What does "inappropriate" behavior look like? Further, the notion of "social maladjustment" as an exclusionary clause has generated much controversy over the years. Some (e.g., Nelson, 1992) have argued that the exclusionary clause is no different than the criterion that defines ED and is therefore illogical. Others (e.g., Skiba & Grizzle, 1991) have argued that rather than being illogical, the social maladjustment clause was essentially a legislative accident made when the law was first passed in 1975. More on the topic of social maladjustment and its relationship to the concept of emotional disturbance is described next.

Definitions of Social Maladjustment

The term *social maladjustment* (SM) was first introduced by Samuel Kirk in 1962 (Hughes et al., 2008). In 1975, the term was added as an exclusionary clause for the category of emotional disturbance by Congress in Public Law 94-142 to avoid providing special education services to juvenile delinquents (Hughes et al., 2008; Skiba & Grizzle, 1991). However, since 1975 no substantial changes to the definition of emotional disturbance have been made. Indeed, the most recent reauthorization of *IDEIA* continues to retain social maladjustment as an exclusionary clause when determining if a child is ED (Hughes et al., 2008).

Unfortunately, the operational definition has been and remains elusive. In fact, social maladjustment is not defined in *IDEIA*. This has led to a variety of responses, including ignoring the requirement to distinguish between ED and SM. Although the issue of ED and SM has been discussed extensively in the context of conduct disorders, it has not yet – and may never – become an issue in the context of NSSI. Indeed, there are currently no data available describing the percentage of students who have been classified as having an emotional disturbance as a result of engaging in NSSI, although this number is presumably small. For more information on ED and social maladjustment and their implications for psychoeducational classification, the reader is referred to Hughes and colleagues (2008).

Psychoeducational Classification and the Medical Model

A significant problem with many current diagnostic systems, including both the *DSM* and *IDEIA*, is that they often convey and reinforce the notion that disorders and disabilities lie within the individual; more specifically, they represent a *medical model* of conceptualizing academic, social, emotional, and/or behavioral problems (Gutkin, 2009). Although certain problems in children and youth clearly do have biological causes that require medical interventions, many psychological and mental health conditions are neither caused nor maintained, either exclusively or primarily, by biological variables. Nevertheless, school personnel often assume, likely in large part because under current diagnostic systems students are classified as essentially "having" particular disorders or handicapping conditions, that the problems exhibited are frequently (even typically) manifestations of variables within the student (e.g., a student will be described as "having" an emotional disturbance, or that he or she "is" emotionally disturbed). As a result, psychological disorders and problems will often be interpreted as having a medical cause and therefore requiring a medical treatment, or the problems are seen as resulting from internal conditions in the students themselves (e.g., lack of "will power," deficits in "character") rather than any ecological forces or conditions outside the student (Gutkin, 2009).

Such interpretations often lead to what Steege and Watson (2009) describe as "the blame game," that is, essentially blaming the student for his or her disorder or disability and, by extension, removing the responsibility of school personnel for its treatment. These authors provide the following example of "the blame game" and how it can affect the behavior of school practitioners:

> Consider the case of the 15-year-old student who has been recently diagnosed with an anxiety disorder. In this case, the diagnosis was provided by an outside mental health clinic. After reviewing the reports from the clinic, individualized education program (IEP) team members breathed a sigh of relief and said: "Well, there's not much we can do about that. Anxiety is a medical condition. That explains why she has been struggling in school. Until the anxiety is addressed, there is nothing we can do." (p. 2)

In this case, a mental health problem (anxiety) often caused and/or maintained by cognitive and/or environmental variables, is conceptualized as a medical problem caused and/or maintained by biological variables. More significantly, although this problem could be treated, and in most cases would best be treated, by evidence-based psychosocial interventions (e.g., environmental modifications, cognitive-behavior therapy), this will likely not occur, largely because the way in which the nature of the problem – and therefore its possible treatment – is conceptualized.

Going Beyond Special Education Eligibility Determination

In concluding this discussion of educationally handicapping conditions in general and emotional disturbance in particular, it is important for school personnel to be cognizant that the primary purpose of special education eligibility determination is not to "diagnose" or "classify" a student, but rather to begin the process of providing students with effective treatments for their identified problems (Fogt, Miller, & Zirkel, 2003; Miller & Sawka-Miller, 2008). As noted by Prasse (2002), the assessment of students for classification and eligibility purposes "created an unintended outcome of testing for this purpose rather than for obtaining relevant information to guide and inform" academic and behavioral interventions for identified problems (p. 71). As such, it behooves all school personnel to recognize that special education eligibility decisions are only the beginning – and not always a necessary beginning – of the role school personnel have in providing students with appropriate supports in the form of socially valid and empirically supported interventions (Miller & Sawka-Miller, 2008).

In the case of a student exhibiting NSSI, just because a student meets eligibility criteria for a particular classification category (e.g., emotional disturbance) does not mean that student should automatically be classified. Rather, a number of variables have to be considered in making this decision, the most important of which is the degree to which the possible benefits of classification outweigh the possible negative ramifications of this decision. Clearly, decisions to classify a student as in need of special education services due to the presence of NSSI should be made carefully, cautiously, and on an individual, case-by-case basis.

A Problem-Solving Approach to Assessment

In many cases, the school-based professionals responsible for conducting student assessments of NSSI will be school psychologists. Historically, the field of school psychology has been dominated by an assessment role tied largely to special education, particularly diagnostic or classification decisions and special education eligibility determination, otherwise known as the "refer–test–place" model of service delivery. However, in recent decades there has been a "paradigm shift" (Reschly, 2008) in the field that has led to a greater emphasis on assessment for purposes of problem solving and data-based decision making rather than diagnostic classification (Ervin, Gimpel Peacock, & Merrell, 2010; Gimpel Peacock, Ervin, Daly, & Merrell, 2010; Merrell, Ervin, & Gimpel, 2006). For example, according to the *Blueprint for Training and Practice in School Psychology III* (Ysseldyke et al., 2006) published by the National Association of School Psychologists (NASP), school psychologists should possess the "ability to use problem-solving and scientific methodology to create, evaluate, and apply appropriately empirically validated interventions at both an individual and a systems level" (p. 14). Moreover, they should be "good problem solvers who collect information that is relevant for understanding problems, make decisions about appropriate interventions, assess educational outcomes, and help become accountable for the decisions they make" (pp. 17–18).

Tilly (2008) concisely summarized the problem-solving process into a four-stage model: (1) What is the problem? (2) Why is it occurring? (3) What can be done about it? and (4) Did it work? In other words, a problem is first identified, possible reasons for why the problem is occurring are identified, an (evidence-based) intervention is designed to address the problem, and the intervention is evaluated to determine whether or not it successfully resolved the problem. As such, a problem-solving approach to assessment focuses on behaviors that are amenable to change, identifies and defines these behaviors in a specific and concrete manner so they can be accurately measured, and uses data to monitor the effectiveness of particular interventions (Ervin et al., 2010).

A problem-solving approach to assessment has been applied by school psychologists and other school-based assessment specialists in a variety of domains, including academic skills such as reading (Marcotte & Hintze, 2010), math (Burns & Klingbeil, 2010), and written expression (Gansle & Noell, 2010) as well as social–emotional and behavioral problems, including both externalizing (Martens & Ardoin, 2010) and internalizing disorders (Miller, 2010). This same approach can, and in our view should, be applied to the school-based assessment of NSSI. For this to occur, school-based mental health professionals need to become knowledgeable and skilled in linking assessment to intervention, a process that is described below.

Functional Assessment: Linking Assessment to Intervention

The diagnostic assessment systems reviewed in the previous chapter are examples of what is known as a *structuralist* approach to assessment. As noted by Claes and Vandereycken (2007):

> From a structuralist approach (medical-clinical viewpoint), self-injurious behavior is considered as a part of a pathological structure (syndrome) or as the symptom of a disorder. Researchers and clinicians are then looking for "typical" features self-injuring patients have in common with other patients with a similar disorder. In the structuralist approach, we are dealing with the question whether SIB needs to be considered as a distinct syndrome or as a symptom of another disorder. (p. 141)

A structuralist approach to assessment focuses on the *topography* or *form* of behavior. In contrast, a *functionalist* or *functional* approach to assessment is "considered as an expression of distress (communicative function) or as a way of coping with distress (problem-solving)" (Claes & Vandereycken, 2007, p. 142). From a functional perspective, the focus is not on diagnostic issues per se, but rather on the contextual and idiographic nature of the problem. Or, in more practical terms, "discerning why this particular behavior, at this particular time, is serving this particular function, for this particular person." (Claes & Vandereycken, 2007, p. 142). The primary advantage of a functional approach to assessment is that, in contrast to many diagnostic assessment approaches, it can be more useful for suggesting particular interventions. The primary purpose of a functional assessment is to gather assessment information that can be useful in effectively treating the problem.

Many school-based mental health professionals, particularly school psychologists, have become increasingly familiar with a particular type of functional assessment known as *functional behavioral assessment* (FBA; Jones & Wickstrom, 2010; Steege & Watson, 2009). An FBA may be defined as "a collection of methods for gathering information about antecedents, behaviors, and consequences in order to determine the reason (function) of behavior" (Gresham, Watson, & Skinner, 2001, p. 158). This assessment approach, which emphasizes the effects of environmental contingencies on behavior, is derived from the science of behavior known as applied behavior analysis (Jones & Wickstrom, 2010). The conceptual foundations for functional behavioral assessment were established decades ago by B. F. Skinner. The quote by Skinner (1938) below, originally published in his first book over 70 years ago, concisely summarizes his perspective on the importance of assessing functional relationships:

> Once in possession of a set of terms we may proceed to a kind of description of behavior by giving a running account of a sample of behaviors as it unfolds itself in some frame of reference. . .It may be classified as a narration. . .From data obtained in this way it is possible to classify different kinds of behavior and to determine relative frequencies of appearance. But although this is, properly speaking, a description of behavior, it is not a science in the accepted sense. We need to go beyond mere observation to a study of functional relationships. We need to establish laws by virtue of which we may predict behavior, and we may do this only by finding variables of which behavior is a function. (p. 8)

A functional behavioral assessment is therefore concerned primarily with descriptions of behavior, not for diagnostic or classification purposes, but rather to identify its function(s). When functions of particular behavioral problems are identified, this information can better inform the use of appropriate interventions. That is, functional behavioral assessment can be useful for more effectively linking assessment to treatment.

Functional behavioral assessment methodologies have demonstrated particular utility for assessing child and adolescent disruptive problem behaviors (including self-injurious behaviors) associated with autism and other developmental disabilities (Brock, Jimerson, & Hansen, 2006). Although to date functional assessment has been used primarily in the assessment of externalizing problems (Martens & Ardoin, 2010), recent research suggests that a functional approach can be useful in linking assessment to intervention for many internalizing behavior problems as well, such as school phobia. In fact, functional assessment procedures have demonstrated that what is commonly referred to as "school phobia" may in many instances not be a phobia per se, but rather a form of school refusal (Kearney, Eisen, & Silverman, 1995) or some other problem, such as separation anxiety disorder (Kearney, 2001). For example, possible reasons a student may be absent from school include anxiety related to social aspects of schooling (e.g., public speaking), anxiety about separating from one's parents/caregivers, oppositional and noncompliant behavior, and/or negative parental or school influences (Kearney, 2003). Although one student could refuse to attend school because of performance anxiety related to public speaking, and another could refuse to attend school because of fears about being bullied, in both cases the function of the behavior would be the same – escape or avoidance.

Further, although the function of the behavior in both of these scenarios would be the same, the recommended treatments for each would be different based on the unique environmental contingencies operating to cause and maintain the avoidance behaviors. In the first case, directly working with the student and providing interventions in relaxation training, skills training in public speaking, and cognitive restructuring might be useful (Miller, 2010). In the second case, rather than focusing on the student, treatment might emphasize better monitoring by school staff of areas in which the student is likely to be bullied, such as the playground or cafeteria.

In contrast, another student may engage in school refusal behavior not as the result of experiencing anxiety, but rather because the student is allowed to stay home and watch television when he or she claims to be sick. In this situation – which is more accurately described as school refusal behavior rather than school phobia – the behavior is maintained as a result of positive reinforcement (i.e., obtaining the desired activity of watching television) rather than escape/avoidance of an aversive environmental event (Miller, 2010). As the above scenarios illustrate, functional behavioral assessment can be useful for assessing those environmental contingencies that are causing or maintaining problem behaviors. In using this assessment approach, identifying the topography (i.e., description) of behavior is still important, but not as important as identifying possible functions of the behavior.

Functional assessment methodologies, which include interviews and direct observations, can be highly useful, particularly if the problem behaviors are frequent and can be readily observed (as in school refusal). In particular, an essential component of most functional behavioral assessments is the use of direct observations through a narrative, ABC (antecedents–behavior–consequence) analysis. An ABC analysis allows the assessor to observe the problem behavior in its actual environmental context, and is based on direct observations of behavior rather than retrospective (and possibly inaccurate) reports about those behaviors. Consequently, using functional behavioral assessment methodologies have been particularly useful for assessing disruptive, acting-out, externalizing behavior problems that easily lend themselves to direct observation, and school psychologists in particular should be knowledgeable and skilled in this area (see Steege & Watson, 2009, for a comprehensive guide to conducting FBAs). However, with many child and adolescent internalizing problems in which problem behaviors are more covert and less likely to be directly observed – such as NSSI – the direct observation of problem behavior is not likely to be as useful. In such instances, student interviews and self-reports become much more critical in the functional assessment process.

Finally, although functional behavioral assessment is primarily concerned with assessing environmental affects on behavior, its scope can be broadened to include other variables as well (Miller, 2010). When conducting a functional assessment of NSSI, for optimum results Walsh (2006) recommends that mental health professionals assess the five interrelated dimensions of his biopsychosocial model of self-injury, described in Chapter 2. Procedures for conducting a comprehensive, functional assessment of NSSI, and linking this information to the formulation of effective treatment strategies, is described next.

The Cognitive-Behavioral Assessment of NSSI in Schools

The purpose of a functional assessment of NSSI is to provide a more complete understanding of the behavior and its function, so that appropriate treatments can be implemented to address it. Before this process can begin, the school-based mental health professional conducting the assessment should be generally familiar with self-injury in youth, including its causes (as described in Chapter 2), its prevalence and associated conditions (as described in Chapter 3), screening and referral procedures (as described in Chapter 4), recommended diagnostic and assessment practices (as described in Chapter 5 and in this chapter), and finally how to effectively respond to and treat NSSI (as described next in Chapter 7). Assuming this has occurred, a functional assessment of NSSI should begin by first having the referred student describe the most recent incident of self-injury, and to do so in a nonthreatening manner that elicits the youth's perspective (Heath & Nixon, 2009). The assessment should also be conducted in such a way that promotes a positive and therapeutic alliance with the student, as discussed in the previous chapter. A primary goal of the psychoeducational assessment process is to better understand the scope and severity of the behavior, as well as conduct a functional assessment through examining and analyzing the multiple variables that may be contributing to self-injury.

In conducting a comprehensive functional assessment of NSSI, Walsh's (2006) cognitive-behavioral approach would appear to have particular utility for school-based mental health professionals, and will be the primary model described in this chapter. The model addresses five interconnected areas that can be helpful in better understanding and treating self-injury, including environmental, biological, cognitive, affective, and behavioral. Assessment begins with the behavioral dimension because (a) it is important to evaluate the specifics of NSSI at the outset, and (b) so the clinician can help to identify those conditions that precede, precipitate, follow, and maintain the behavior (Walsh, 2006). This involves a three-step process of collecting measurable data and descriptive information about (1) the *antecedents* to self-injury; (2) the *behavior* itself; and (3) the immediate *consequences* of engaging in NSSI. To begin this process, Walsh recommends the use of a self-injury log.

Self-Injury Log

One way to collect information regarding NSSI is to ask students engaging in it to complete a self-injury log. This log is a grid that contains a listing of several categories across each day of the week. Although the log is most useful initially to get a baseline assessment of the student's current NSSI behaviors and where and when they are most likely to occur, it can also be used repeatedly thereafter to monitor student progress in treatment. Students who are identified as engaging in NSSI and receive subsequent treatment for it are then encouraged to record entries in their self-injury log on a daily basis. Categories that may be included in a self-injury log include the kind of physical damage caused by the self-injury, the instrument used to inflict the damage, the extent of the damage, the area on the body where the damage was inflicted, the pattern of the wounds (i.e., the visual arrangement of wounds inflicted during a single episode of NSSI), the room or place in which the NSSI occurred, and the social context (i.e., whether the person engaged in NSSI alone or with another person or other persons) of the behavior. For more information on self-injury logs, including an example of one, the reader is referred to Walsh (2006).

Antecedents to NSSI

Once the details of the self-injury have been assessed, the school mental health practitioner can address the issue of antecedents across the five dimensions listed below.

Environmental antecedents. These are defined as "events or activities in the environment of the self-injurer that trigger an episode" (Walsh, 2006, p. 96). It is critical to assess what particular environmental events preceded and set the self-injuring sequence in motion. Once identified, these environmental antecedents can provide targets for intervention, as they provide opportunities to learn and practice healthier and more appropriate behaviors in place of NSSI. External events that are commonly cited by individuals as precipitating NSSI episodes include (a) loss or threat of loss of a relationship with a significant other; (b) interpersonal conflict; (c) performance pressures; (d) frustration occurring as a result of unmet needs; (e) social isolation; and (f) seemingly neutral events that trigger associations with trauma (Walsh, 2006).

Environmental antecedents that trigger self-injury will often occur in close proximity in time (e.g., immediately or just before an episode of NSSI takes place), but this is not always the case. Some antecedents may not be temporally proximal to the behavior of interest, and may also influence behavior change by momentarily altering the effectiveness of reinforcing consequences (Steege & Watson, 2009). Known as *establishing operations* (Jones & Wickstrom, 2010) or *motivating operations* (Laraway, Snycerski, Michael, & Poling, 2003), it is important to determine if these may be a factor when conducting a functional assessment of NSSI.

For example, the first author was involved in the assessment of an adolescent girl who was engaging in self-injury during the school day. The girl attended an alternative day school for students with severe emotional and behavioral disorders. Her parents were divorced; she lived with her mother and visited her father every other weekend. A functional assessment of the girl's NSSI behavior indicated that it typically occurred on Mondays, but only those Mondays immediately following weekends spent with her father. In an interview with the girl, she revealed that her feelings for her father were emotionally ambivalent; she reported loving and missing him, but also expressed severe anger at him for leaving her mother and for developing a romantic relationship with another woman. In this case, it appeared that weekend visits with her father were functioning as a motivating operation for self-injury; her NSSI was not actually exhibited until after these visits and she returned to school, where she also received attention from her peers for her wounds. It was hypothesized that what happened to the student over the weekend increased the motivation she had to obtain reinforcement (in this case attention) through NSSI behaviors.

This case example also illustrates another important point regarding functional assessment. Specifically, the functions underlying behavior are not in and of themselves problematic, but rather the manner in which these functions are achieved. In the case example described above, it is not the student's desire for attention from others that is a problem, but rather the manner in which she attempts to access attention (i.e., via engaging in NSSI).

Biological antecedents. These refer to chronic physical problems, physical vulnerabilities, or more immediate physical concerns (Walsh, 2006). Of perhaps greatest significance in the context of assessing NSSI is that many forms of mental illness, such as depression, bipolar disorder, schizophrenia, and borderline personality disorder, are believed to have a strong biological component. Many individuals who engage in NSSI have mental health problems that contribute to it, and possible "triggers" that may precipitate a self-injury episode include biological ones. For example, short-term triggers may include fatigue, over- or under-eating, excessive exercise, insomnia, and the abuse of alcohol or drugs. Other common and more immediate triggers may include failure to comply with prescribed medications or abuse of medications (Walsh, 2006). Walsh recommends that individuals who engage in recurrent episodes of NSSI should be assessed for

- emotional dysregulation (which may respond to anticonvulsant medications)
- depression, anxiety, and impulsive aggression (which may respond to an SSRI or other form of medication)
- addiction to the release of endogenous opioids associated with NSSI (which may respond to naltrexone)
- diminished sensitivity to physical pain (for which there is no known pharmacological treatment).

Each of these areas can be important biological contributors to NSSI, and should be assessed to determine their level and degree of contributions to the problem.

Cognitive antecedents. These refer to particular thoughts and beliefs that may precede episodes of NSSI. Based on Beck's (1995) cognitive model, these may include (a) interpretations of external events; (b) automatic thoughts; (c) intermediate beliefs; (d) core beliefs; and (e) cognitions and other mental activity related to trauma. The cognitive interpretation and evaluation of events, automatic thoughts, and other cognitive variables often occur immediately prior to acts of self-injury, and it is therefore critically important to assess if this is occurring in students exhibiting NSSI.

Affective antecedents. These refer to the emotions experienced by an individual before engaging in NSSI. In some cases, emotions can build over a sustained period of time (e.g., several days) prior to self-injury, while for others emotional reactions can occur in an instant. For most individuals who engage in NSSI, its purpose appears to be the reduced intensity of painful emotions. Some examples of painful emotions that might, under certain circumstances, increase the probability of NSSI include (a) anxiety, tension, or panic; (b) anger; (c) sadness or depression; (d) shame; (e) guilt; (f) frustration; and (g) contempt. A smaller proportion of self-injurers report engaging in this behavior not because they experience too much emotion, but because they experience too little of it. For these individuals, who report feeling emotionally "dead" or "empty," engaging in NSSI appears to enhance their level, degree, and/or intensity of emotional experience (Walsh, 2006).

Behavioral antecedents. These refer to observable actions by students that trigger self-injury episodes and are key variables in the sequence that culminates in self-injury. Many individuals develop a predictable pattern of when they are most likely to engage in NSSI, with certain behaviors often immediately or closely preceding episodes of self-injury. Walsh (2006) provides some examples of behavioral antecedents to NSSI, including (a) intoxication due to alcohol or being high on marijuana or other drugs; (b) the discontinuation of prescribed medication for mental health issues; (c) overeating, and then feeling disgusted for doing so; and (d) behaving in a way an individual finds personally embarrassing. Although each of the above behavioral antecedents includes thoughts and feelings that accompany them, the behaviors themselves can be the key element that triggers the self-injury. If the assessor does not know the specific behavioral antecedents, the cognitive and affective antecedents will also frequently not be adequately identified. As such, it is of critical importance to know what the student was specifically *doing* right before episodes of self-injury occur (Walsh, 2006).

Consequences of NSSI

Walsh (2006) recommends that the consequences or aftermath of self-injury should be assessed in several areas, including (a) specifics of the psychological relief; (b) presence or absence of self-care after NSSI; (c) presence or absence of excoriation after the NSSI; (d) presence or absence of communication regarding the NSSI; (e) demeanor of the student describing the NSSI; and (f) social reinforcement.

Specifics of the psychological relief. This refers to the alleviation of psychological pain as a result of engaging in NSSI. The assessor should determine if following self-injury the student experiences a decrease in psychological and emotional distress. If this is the case, it is also important to know the specific type of relief the NSSI provides, because the positive replacement behaviors, which would be a part of treatment, should essentially "mimic" this type of relief. For example, if the student states that engaging in NSSI leads to feelings of deep relaxation, treatment should focus on activities that lead to increased relaxation. If the student claims that self-injury produces peaceful sleep, the treatment might focus on sleep-induction techniques. Or, if the student indicates that he or she engages in self-injury in response to experiencing high levels of anger and frustration, the treatment approach might emphasize teaching the student anger management techniques (Walsh, 2006).

Presence or absence of self-care after NSSI. This refers to whether or not the student attends to wounds after acts of self-injury. Some students may take at least basic sanitary precautions to ensure their wounds do not become infected, while others may provide little or no self-care to wounds or may even deliberately attempt to induce infection. For students who take little or no care to address their wounds, this may represent an extension of their self-harming behavior, and if serious enough indicates a severe enough level of student distress and pathology to warrant the need for assessment for possible hospitalization (Walsh, 2006).

Presence or absence of excoriation after NSSI. This refers to whether or not the student deliberately opens wounds after episodes of self-injury. Failure to adequately care for wounds represents a passive form of self-injury, whereas excoriation indicates an active form. If a student repeatedly opens the same wound located in the same area, the assessor should attempt to determine the meaning this particular body area may have for the individual, as this may provide important clues about why and where the NSSI is occurring (Walsh, 2006).

Presence or absence of communication after NSSI. This refers to whether or not the student chooses to inform others about the self-injury after it occurs. It is important to assess this to determine if the NSSI is primarily intrapersonally oriented or at least partly serves an interpersonal communication function. Although most individuals who engage in NSSI do so when they are alone, most also disclose it to a small number of people after it occurs. Although in most case NSSI may be driven primarily by internal psychological distress, it may also be intended secondarily to communicate to others. The assessor should attempt to discover both the content of the "message" being communicated via self-injury and the intended recipient of that message (Walsh, 2006).

Demeanor of the student describing NSSI. This refers to the behavior of the student self-injurer when describing or exhibiting his or her wounds. The demeanor of the student as observed by the assessor often conveys substantial information about the student's motivation to stop, or at least decrease, the frequency of self-injury. Some students may express remorse or shame, suggesting a motivation to get help; others may express an open defiance of disapproval by others, suggesting the student is not currently motivated to change; still others may express bland disinterest. When assessing students suspected of engaging in NSSI, it is best to put aside assumptions or preconceptions and listen carefully to the student without judgment; a skill that sounds simple enough but is often difficult to put into practice (Walsh, 2006).

Social reinforcement. This refers to behavior on the part of other persons in the student's environment that increases the likelihood of NSSI recurring (Walsh, 2006). Any sort of attention provided in response to self-injury may reinforce the behavior, regardless of the manner in which the attention is provided. For example, a peer who compliments a student for engaging in NSSI is providing one form of attention that would clearly be considered inappropriate and counterproductive. On the other hand, school personnel and others should be cognizant that engaging in behaviors designed to "help" people with self-injury may inadvertently reinforce it by providing attention to the student engaging in it (which is why school personnel are encouraged to exhibit a low-key, dispassionate demeanor when responding to self-injury). Additionally, it is equally important for school personnel to recognize that obtaining social reinforcement is seldom the primary motivator (i.e., function) of NSSI, although it can be a prominent *secondary* motivator. Almost all people, including youth, who engage in NSSI experience a high degree of psychological distress. The notion that people engage in self-injury primarily to "get attention" is untrue and not supported by empirical evidence. Nevertheless, the potential for youth who self-injure to receive social reinforcement for it is very real, a situation made even more troubling by the Internet.

Assessing the Role of the Internet in Student Self-Injury

An area for assessment that has become increasingly important in recent years is the relationship between the Internet and students who self-injure. Nearly 90% of American youth between the ages of 12 and 17 years use the Internet regularly, and more than half do so on a daily basis (Whitlock, Lader, & Conterio, 2007). The Internet provides opportunities for information gathering and social interaction on a scale unprecedented in human history. For adolescents in particular, the Internet (and its offshoots, such as instant messaging) is used primarily for social reasons; Web sites such as myspace.com have surpassed shopping malls as the primary socializing venue for teenagers in the United States (Whitlock et al., 2007). A form of communication with nearly unlimited possibilities that did not even exist until a few years ago, the Internet now allows students with NSSI to develop a rapid (and perhaps artificial) identification with others, in which students can share their histories, experiences, and practices (Whitlock et al., 2007).

Like other stigmatized behaviors (e.g., anorexia nervosa), self-injury communities and outlets are highly prevalent on the Internet. Online communication may be particularly appealing to adolescent self-injurers because the assurance of anonymity is likely comforting to individuals struggling with a variety of negative emotions and cognitions, including shame and psychological distress (McKenna & Bargh, 2000; Whitlock et al., 2006). A recent study found that online interactions on self-injury message boards provide therapeutic social support for otherwise isolated adolescents. In particular, informal supports and online discussions of proximal life events that triggered self-injury were the most common types of communication exchanges, followed by casual and occasionally personal information related to the addictive qualities of NSSI, fears about disclosing their self-injury to others, counseling and psychotherapy experiences, the methods they used to self-injure, and other related health concerns. Unfortunately, this same study found that Internet sites may also have the effect of normalizing and even encouraging self-injurious behavior, as well as adding potentially lethal behaviors to the repertoire of established adolescent self-injurers (Whitlock et al., 2006).

Whitlock and colleagues (2007) recommend that mental health practitioners become familiar with popular Internet sites devoted to self-injury, including those sites that actively promote NSSI. They also recommend that they assess the student's use of the Internet in general and self-injury focused Internet sites in particular, both during the initial assessment and throughout the treatment process. Whitlock and colleagues suggest asking the following general questions about the Internet:

- "How often do you visit the Internet to get or share health information?"
- "Have you ever made friends over the Internet?" (p. 1140)

Regarding the student's use of the Internet specifically in the context of NSSI, Whitlock and colleagues (2007) suggest asking the student if he or she has ever visited a Web site to find out about or discuss self-injury. If the answer to this question is affirmative, Whitlock and colleagues suggest asking the following follow-up questions:

- "Are there places you regularly go to find out about or to talk about self-injury?"
- "How often do you visit this/these site(s)?"
- "What do you like to do most while there?"
- "Do you like to post messages (or videos) or do you like just to see what is happening?"
- "What type of site(s) do you visit?"
- "Can you tell me the name of the sites you like the best?" (p. 1141)

If the responses to these questions indicate that the student is a regular and frequent visits to self-injury websites, Whitlock and colleagues (2007) suggest that the following additional questions may prove beneficial:

- "How close do you consider your Internet friends to be?"
- "Have you ever met with friends you made online?"
- "How comfortable do you feel hearing stories from others who self-injure?"
- "Have you shared your own story? How did this feel?"
- "What do you like most about having friends that you only really know through the Internet?"
- "How honest are you when you share information on the Web?" (Do you minimize or tend to embellish?)
- "Do you tend to remain anonymous, or do you share your name and contact information?" (p. 1141)

Finally, if students are developing online relationships with others on the Internet who may be strongly influencing their own self-perceptions and behavior, it is important to assess the nature, extent, and effect of these relationships. Whitlock and colleagues (2007) suggest the following questions can be useful in this context:

- "Do you have Internet friends with whom you talk about self-injury?"
- "Do you ever take their advice?"
- "Can you provide examples of advice you got from an Internet friend that you used?" (p. 1141)

The Internet is a powerful communication and information-sharing tool that is now pervasive in the lives of most Americans, particularly American youth. For those students who engage in NSSI, the Internet can provide "a means of expressing suppressed feelings and of connecting with others like themselves" (Whitlock et al., 2007, p. 1142). As such, the nature, extent, and effect of the Internet on these students should be assessed by appropriate school personnel, and the results of this assessment may have important implications for treatment.

Concluding Comments

In discussing assessment in general and functional behavioral assessment in particular, Gresham (2009) offered the cogent opinion that "the only good assessment is one that results in an effective intervention" (p. vii). Although psychoeducational and other forms of assessment have a number of purposes, none are more important than providing information that can be used to help students with particular problems they may be experiencing and/or exhibiting. In the context of NSSI, conducting a comprehensive assessment within a cognitive-behavioral framework can be useful for identifying potentially effective treatments. The structure of this assessment should focus first on creating a therapeutic alliance with the student, and thereafter on the history and specifics of the behavior and its intrapersonal and/or interpersonal function(s) for the student (Walsh, 2007). To support effective intervention efforts, school-based mental health professionals are encouraged to use this approach when assessing students who may be engaging in NSSI. A discussion of how school personnel can most effectively respond to, and provide treatment for, students who self-injure is provided in Chapter 7.

Chapter 7
Treatment

At a minimum, school-based mental health professionals must be able to identify and assess students who may be engaging in NSSI, and either directly provide or (more likely) facilitate effective intervention and treatment. Because the school will in many instances not be the ideal or most appropriate treatment setting for students engaging in NSSI, and because school personnel may lack the training and experience to provide comprehensive school-based interventions, the first part of this chapter is on prevention issues as well as how school personnel can effectively respond to students engaging in NSSI and coordinate or collaborate with others so that students receive the necessary treatment for their self-injury.

In reviewing treatments for NSSI, a school-based, public health approach to prevention and intervention is provided, including a review of interventions provided at universal, selected, and tertiary levels. School-wide prevention strategies and preparedness are discussed, as well as more individualized interventions for students identified as engaging in NSSI and the issue of possible contagion effects in schools. Although it is generally not expected that school-based mental health practitioners will be the providers of direct treatment of students engaging in NSSI through psychosocial interventions such as psychotherapy, it is important that these professionals have a general understanding of evidence-based treatments for it, particularly to guide students and their parents or caregivers to more appropriate treatment options. Similarly, school personnel should have a general understanding regarding the current knowledge base regarding the psychopharmacological treatment of NSSI, and a brief overview of this treatment option is provided as well. This chapter begins with a summary of pertinent ethical, legal, and social justice considerations, as these issues are critical for understanding the responsibilities school personnel have in responding to self-harm in youth.

Responding to NSSI in Schools: Ethical, Legal, and Social Justice Issues

As noted in Chapter 1, school personnel have an ethical and legal duty to protect students from reasonably foreseeable risk of harm, including self-harm (Jacob &

D.N. Miller, S.E. Brock, *Identifying, Assessing, and Treating Self-Injury at School*,
Developmental Psychopathology at School, DOI 10.1007/978-1-4419-6092-4_7,
© Springer Science+Business Media, LLC 2010

Hartshorne, 2007). That is, school personnel have an ethical and legal obligation to make reasonable and prudent efforts to prevent foreseeable self-harm whenever possible. However, as noted by Berman (2009): "Foreseeability is not synonymous with predictability. Rather, foreseeability refers to a reasonable assessment of a student's risk for potential harm" (p. 234). In addition, school personnel should not be negligent in responding to clear cases of NSSI. Clearly, school personnel cannot be held accountable for inadequately responding to a student's self-injury if they do not know it is occurring. However, in situations in which school personnel are aware of a student's self-injury, or even if they suspect this possibility, they have an obligation to share this information with an appropriate school-based mental health professional.

When working with students suspected of engaging in NSSI, school personnel should always engage in appropriate ethical and legal behavior for a variety of reasons, including helping the student in need, complying with ethical and legal requirements, and maintaining professional standards. Froeschle and Moyer (2004), Lieberman and Poland (2006), and Lieberman, Toste, and Heath (2009) provide some useful recommendations to school-based mental health professional in these areas, including (a) recognize the limits of your skills and abilities; (b) maintain accurate and objective records; (c) become familiar with any pertinent federal or state laws; (d) become familiar with school and district policies and procedures; (e) collaborate and confer with colleagues; (f) maintain liability insurance coverage; and (g) discuss with school administrators their level of awareness and support of the above issues. Additionally, because youth who engage in NSSI may first come to the attention of school personnel in a variety of different contexts (e.g., assessment, treatment), school-based mental health professionals should be prepared to inform students of the limits of confidentiality during situations in which NSSI is first suspected or disclosed.

Moreover, given that many youth are minors and in the custody of their parents or caregivers, school personnel are ethically and legally obligated to contact parents if a student presents an immediate threat to him- or herself or others. As was acknowledged in Chapter 4, while this is a straightforward and unambiguous procedure if the student is engaging in potentially suicidal behavior, if it is determined that a student is engaging in NSSI but is not imminently suicidal, the appropriate ethical and legal response becomes less clear. In general, it is best practice to involve parents or caregivers at all times if it is determined their child is engaging in or suspected of engaging in self-injury. In fact, school personnel may be in legal jeopardy for nondisclosure if a student who reports NSSI is later seriously injured or dies (Lieberman & Poland, 2006). That said, not all students who have engaged in NSSI *must* have their parents or guardians contacted. School personnel should be cognizant of state or provincial laws regarding the school's legal obligation to contact parents or caregivers and under what circumstances this should occur (Lieberman et al., 2009). In those situations when parents or caregivers are notified regarding their child's self-injurious behavior, this should be done with "patience, tolerance, and cultural responsiveness" (Lieberman et al., 2009, p. 206).

In addition to the ethical and legal importance of responding appropriately to student self-injury, this issue can also be viewed as a moral one. Although the terms *ethics* and *morality* are often used interchangeably, they are distinctive, in the sense that the term *morality* "refers to a subset of ethical rules of special importance" (Jacob & Hartshorne, 2007. p. 2). Moral principles provide a foundation for the ethical codes of psychologists as well as other professionals (Bersoff & Koeppl, 1993), and among the moral duties of an ethical person is *justice* (Ross, 1930). Justice is concerned with the equitable and fair treatment of individuals and groups, particularly those who are at highest risk for not receiving just treatment, such as those who are or who are likely to be *marginalized* by others with more power and influence in particular environmental contexts.

Like other groups of students, such as students living in poverty (Miller & Sawka-Miller, 2009) and lesbian, gay, bisexual, and transgendered students (McCabe & Robinson, 2008), youth who engage in NSSI are at risk for potentially being discriminated against and marginalized by their peers as well as school staff. In fact, D'Onofrio (2007) has suggested that NSSI may be "a behavioral subtext of a larger social disorder that is characterized by increased alienation and disfranchisement – specifically, that within the deep structure of self-injurious behaviors lie issues relating to power imbalances, group marginalization, and social injustice" (p. 30). School-based mental health practitioners are therefore encouraged to adopt a social justice perspective (McCabe & Robinson, 2008; Miller & Sawka-Miller, 2009; Nastasi, 2008; Rogers & O'Bryon, 2008; Shriberg, 2009; Shriberg et al., 2008) in regards to students who engage in NSSI, such as providing education to students and staff about this condition, working to implement just policies and procedures in responding to students who self-injure, and advocating on their behalf at both individual and systemic levels.

In summary, all school personnel have a duty to protect students from reasonably foreseeable risk of harm (Jacob, 2009). This includes self-harm, such as suicidal behavior and NSSI. Although protecting students from self-harming behaviors is certainly a commendable and appropriate goal for school personnel, to do this most effectively it is necessary to consider not just treating problems when they occur, but also minimizing the probability of their initial development. That is, efforts must be made at preventing problems as well as treating them. One approach that combines prevention and intervention is known as a public health model.

A Public Health Perspective on Preventing and Treating NSSI in Schools

A central characteristic of a public health approach is its emphasis on prevention and early intervention with entire populations rather than individuals (Doll & Cummings, 2008; Gutkin, 2009; Strein, Hoagwood, & Cohn, 2003). A public health approach as applied in schools can perhaps best be conceptualized using Gordon's (1983) and Walker and colleagues' (1996) three-tiered model, which includes three overlapping tiers that collectively represent a continuum of interventions that increase in intensity to meet individual student needs (Sugai, 2007). The first tier is referred to as the *universal* level, because all students in a given population (e.g., school, classroom) are recipients of interventions designed to prevent particular problems. The second tier, commonly referred to as the *selected* level, comprises more intensive interventions for those students who do not adequately respond to universal interventions. The third and final tier, referred to as the *indicated* or *tertiary* level, is characterized by highly individualized interventions for those students who do not respond adequately to universal or selected levels of prevention and intervention.

A public health approach to prevention and intervention is increasingly viewed as an important educational practice (Merrell et al., 2006; Ysseldyke et al., 2006). It has been advocated for a variety of problems in schools (Miller, Eckert, & Mazza, 2009), including the prevention and treatment of antisocial behavior (Horner, Sugai, Todd, & Lewis-Palmer, 2005); aggression and bullying (Swearer, Espelage, Brey Love, & Kingsbury, 2008); child poverty (Miller & Sawka-Miller, 2009); academic problems (Martinez & Nellis, 2008); social and emotional problems (Merrell, Gueldner, & Tran, 2008); substance abuse problems (Burrows-Sanchez & Hawken, 2007); and internalizing problems (Levitt & Merrell, 2009), including depression (Mazza & Reynolds, 2008) and suicide (Miller, in press; Miller, Eckert, & Mazza, 2009). Such an approach could also be potentially useful in the school-based prevention and treatment of NSSI.

School-Based Prevention of NSSI: Universal Strategies

Possible components of a universal approach include a focus on increasing awareness of NSSI, providing information regarding risk factors and warning signs, dispelling myths about NSSI, teaching appropriate responses to peers who may come into contact with someone who may exhibit NSSI, and potentially identifying youth who may be at risk for NSSI. Such programs would be presented to all students in a given population regardless of their level of risk, and the key assumption is that the conditions that contribute to the development of NSSI in youth "often go unrecognized, undiagnosed, and untreated, and that educating students and gatekeepers about the appropriate responses will result in better identification of at-risk youth, and an increase in help seeking and referral for treatment" (Hendin et al., 2005, p. 446).

For example, because NSSI in adolescence is often characterized by difficulty in the expression of emotions, self-derogation, anxiety, and poor distress tolerance (Klonsky, 2007; Muehlenkamp, 2006; Walsh, 2006), schools can provide students with needed information on more adaptive methods of coping with these types of problems and stress in general (Lieberman et al., 2009). Specifically, school personnel might offer activities within the curriculum, or teach students stress management and emotional awareness skills. Such programs provide school-based professionals with the opportunity to help youth develop multiple avenues for managing or expressing emotions, and may be potentially useful in preventing some students who would ordinarily engage in NSSI from doing so (Lieberman et al., 2009).

Correcting Myths and Misunderstandings About NSSI

School-based mental health professionals can and should be cognizant of the many myths associated with self-injury. This information, as well as other misinformation or misunderstanding that may surround NSSI, should be clearly communicated on a regular basis (e.g., at least annually) to all students and staff. Kanan and colleagues (2008) and Lieberman and Poland (2006) provide a number of myths associated with NSSI, including (a) all youth who self-injure are suicidal; (b) self-decoration (e.g., tattooing) is self-injury; (c) all youth who engage in self-injury have been physically or sexually abused; (d) all youth who engage in self-injury have borderline personality disorder; (e) all youth who self-injure need to be hospitalized; (f) youth who self-injure use this behavior to manipulate other people; (g) youth who self-injure just want attention; and (h) people who engage in self-injury are dangerous and will probably harm others in addition to themselves.

Promoting Student Strengths and Resiliency

As mentioned previously, schools have an ethical and legal obligation to offer safe and secure environments for all students (Jacob & Hartshorne, 2007), and to provide programs and experiences that foster youth resilience (Lieberman et al., 2009). Schools can better promote student resiliency by emphasizing and providing better access to mental health services, family–school connectedness, limiting access to lethal weapons, encouraging help-seeking behaviors and good relations with peers, and developing students' problem-solving and coping skills (Brock, Sandoval, & Hart, 2006; Lieberman et al., 2009). Schools can become a place where students feel more connected and engaged (Appleton, Christenson, & Furlong, 2008) if school environments are created "where youth are able to express themselves, discuss issues and concerns, engage with peers and adults in a safe space, and seek out resources if they experience difficulties. This connectedness empowers students and serves as a universal strategy for preventing NSSI and other risky behaviors among youth" (Lieberman et al., 2009, p. 197).

A universal approach to NSSI in schools should be concerned not only with preventing NSSI, but also promoting individual student strengths, competencies, and healthy living skills. Consequently, universal prevention programs for NSSI may benefit from incorporating findings from the professional literature on health promotion (Nastasi, 2004; Power, 2003) and the emerging field of positive psychology (Peterson, 2006; Snyder & Lopez, 2007), which is increasingly being applied in schools (Gilman, Huebner, & Furlong, 2009; Miller & Nickerson, 2007b). For example, given that youth who engage in NSSI often experience a high degree of negative emotions and thoughts, teaching skills for the promotion of positive emotions (Fredrickson & Joiner, 2002) and cognitions (Wingate et al., 2006) could be a useful prevention strategy. Further, given that youth who engage in NSSI may experience high levels of social isolation, developing programs designed to enhance students' perceived social support (Demaray & Malecki, 2002) and school connectedness (Appleton et al., 2008) may promote their sense of belongingness, an important variable for addressing both NSSI and suicidal behavior (Joiner, 2005).

Other potential areas for universal prevention programs include teaching students skills related to emotional regulation (Buckley & Saarni, 2009) and promoting hope (Lopez, Rose, Robinson, Marques, & Pais-Ribeiro, 2009), optimism (Boman, Furlong, Shochet, Lilles, & Jones, 2009), and life satisfaction (Suldo, Huebner, Friedrich, & Gilman, 2009). The emphasis within positive psychology on wellness promotion (Miller, Gilman, & Martens, 2008) and increasing competencies rather than merely decreasing problems is strongly aligned with a public health approach to prevention and intervention (Miller et al., 2009).

Although the universal strategies described above may potentially be useful in the prevention of NSSI, to date there have been no studies that have empirically demonstrated this. However, many of these strategies have been recommended as being potentially useful in the prevention of other problems, such as youth suicidal behavior (Miller et al., 2009), and would likely prove useful for the prevention of NSSI as well. In particular, having strong connections to school, whether this occurs through friendships and social connections, structured extracurricular activities (e.g., being on a sports team, being a member of the band, acting in a school play), as a result of academic competence, or for some other reason, appears to be an important variable. For example, Bearman and Moody (2004) found that adolescents were less likely to harm themselves either through NSSI or suicidal behavior if they attended schools where they felt safe, had a greater density of friendship ties with peers, and perceived themselves as being in a more tightly knit school community.

School-Based Intervention: Responding to NSSI

In regards to NSSI and the schools, Lieberman and colleagues (2009) assert that the primary role of school personnel includes (a) being sufficiently aware of the warning signs of NSSI and how to accurately identify it and (b) immediately and effectively responding to students exhibiting self-injury. In particular, these authors suggest that:

> The most effective factor in improving identification of NSSI in schools is improving awareness of the prevalence of the behavior and ensuring that all school personnel are aware that the behavior requires immediate assessment and intervention. (p. 202)

To accomplish this goal most effectively, as was acknowledged in Chapter 4, they recommend that every school have a self-injury protocol, which is an agreement among school staff members about how incidents or reports of NSSI will be handled (Lieberman et al., 2009). Although there can be some flexibility in this protocol,

Lieberman and colleagues suggest that all school policies regarding the response to NSSI should address the following questions:

- When should school personnel report a student suspected of engaging in NSSI?
- To whom should school personnel report NSSI behaviors?
- To what extent are school administrators involved with students who engage in NSSI?
- To what extent are school mental health professionals and the school nurse involved?
- What is the school's policy on parental/caregiver notification and involvement with regard to NSSI?

School policies and procedures in regards to NSSI should be collaboratively developed among school staff members, although it is logical for school-based health (e.g., school nurse) and mental health professionals to take the lead in developing these written documents. Once written policies and procedures are created, these need to be shared with all school staff members. The dissemination of information should not simply be in the form of distributing written policies and procedures, but rather actively training (Sawka, McCurdy, & Mannella, 2002) in this information so that all school personnel thoroughly learn it and ultimately respond to instances of self-injury in an effective, efficient, and consistent manner.

Lieberman and colleagues (2009) suggest that schools establish a crisis team to respond to NSSI. This team can include a variety of professionals involved in school-based mental health assessment and treatment, and ideally they should be trained in first response and intervention for a wide variety of mental health and other problems, including NSSI. Each school should have designated school-based professionals for NSSI referral issues (Lieberman et al., 2009), and these individuals should be members of the crisis team. Although one individual in particular may be assigned this task, others should be available for this duty, given that the primary individual responsible may not always be available.

All members of the school crisis team should be knowledgeable and skilled in both the diagnostic and psychoeducational assessment of NSSI, as well as have a clear understanding of how to initially respond to students engaging in it. Moreover, members of this team should be familiar with treatments that have demonstrated empirical support in reducing NSSI behaviors, even if they do not directly provide this treatment, so they can refer the student to appropriate services in the community. Crisis team members should collaborate and be in frequent contact with appropriate members of the school, community, and the student's family. Finally, they should also be cognizant of community-based mental health professionals, coordinate services as needed, and serve as useful conduits of school crisis prevention and intervention strategies for NSSI as well as other problems. There are several useful resources available to facilitate this learning (e.g., Allen Heath & Sheen, 2005; Brock, 2002a, 2002b, 2006; Brock, Lazarus, & Jimerson, 2002; Brock, Nickerson, Reeves, & Jimerson, 2008;Brock, Nickerson, Reeves, Jimersson et al., 2008; Brock,

Sandoval, & Lewis, 2001; Pitcher & Poland, 1992; Poland & McCormick, 1999; Sandoval, 2002; Sandoval & Brock, 2009).

Contagion and its Prevention in Schools

An important issue for school personnel to consider in responding to and effectively treating NSSI is the issue of *contagion*. This refers to "a sequence of events in which an individual engages in self-injurious behaviors and is imitated by others in the environment" (Lieberman et al., 2009, p. 210). Social contagion, or the spread of NSSI, has been anecdotally reported and appears to be a problem in some schools (Lieberman, 2004; Lieberman et al., 2009; Walsh, 2006). In these situations, multiple students who know each other engage in NSSI within short periods of time (Lieberman et al., 2009; Walsh, 2006). These students often appear to be frequently communicating about NSSI among themselves, and essentially triggering and encouraging the behavior in each other. In some situations, contagion may be both immediate and direct; students may engage in NSSI in each other's presence, and may even share the same tools or implements or take turns injuring each other (Lieberman et al., 2009). When multiple students engage in NSSI in an imitative fashion, it may serve the purpose of building feelings of cohesion among students in the group, cementing particular friendships or romances, and/or gaining acceptance or inclusion into a group (Froeschle & Moyer, 2004; Lieberman et al., 2009).

The dissemination of information about contagion effects to school personnel should be approached carefully when responding to outbreaks of multiple students engaging in NSSI (Lieberman et al., 2009). School personnel are encouraged to avoid school-wide communications in the form of general student assemblies or school-wide announcements. Additionally, when students from a particular peer group are referred together for engaging in self-injury, it is recommended that members of the group be divided among several school staff members and that each student be responded to individually (Lieberman et al., 2009).

Walsh (2006) recommends that school professionals employ three strategies to minimize the risk of contagion. First, reduce communication about self-injury among members of the peer group. School staff members can explain to students that that communicating (e.g., talking, emailing, instant messaging) about self-injury has negative effects on their peers by making NSSI more likely; even students who engage in NSSI without remorse may feel guilty about behaving in a manner that may encourage it among their friends. If this is not effective and contagion effects continue, disciplinary action may be needed for some students, including possible suspension until students agree (in writing) to reduce their contagion-generating behaviors.

Second, Walsh recommends reducing the public exhibition of scars or wounds in schools. If this is an issue, it is first recommended to meet with the self-injuring student alone, and make a direct request to the student to cover the wounds or scars while at school. For students who are not responsive to this request, parents or caregivers should be contacted and requested to provide additional clothing that could be used in case a student's attire on a given day might display wounds or scars. In some cases, students may need to be sent home and directed to return only when they have dressed more appropriately to conceal their injuries.

Finally, Walsh suggests providing psychosocial treatments (e.g., counseling and psychotherapy) individually rather than in groups. Treating NSSI in groups can be potentially dangerous because it runs the risk of triggering further instances of self-injury because of open discussions regarding NSSI antecedents, behaviors, and consequences.

The Psychosocial Treatment of NSSI

Students who are determined to be engaging in NSSI based on the assessment of an appropriate school-based mental health professional should generally be referred to appropriate services outside of the school to receive the most effective treatment. Comprehensive psychosocial interventions for NSSI are frequently complex and typically involve multiple components, including contingency management procedures, replacements skills training, cognitive treatment, body image work, exposure treatments, family-based interventions, and psychopharmacological treatment (Walsh, 2006). School personnel, even highly trained mental health professionals working in the school, will typically not have the necessary knowledge, skills, or experience to provide comprehensive psychosocial interventions for students engaging in NSSI, particularly if students are repetitively engaging in this behavior. Moreover, logistical as well as professional constraints may make interventions by school personnel difficult and unlikely (Lieberman et al., 2009). That said, some school-based mental health professionals may be in a position to provide treatment, and others may need to do so given the lack of community resources in isolated rural settings (assuming, of course, that they have the necessary time, knowledge, skills, and experience to do so). However, even if they are not in a position to provide direct treatment, these professionals should be cognizant of evidence-based treatments for NSSI.

A number of different psychosocial interventions for NSSI have been proposed for both youth and adults (e.g., Brown & Bryan, 2007; Klonsky & Muehlankamp, 2007; Levy, Yeomans, & Diamond, 2007). The standard treatment option for individuals engaging in self-injury has been hospitalization (Muehlenkamp, 2006), but this option is an expensive one and has not demonstrated to be an effective intervention either for suicidal behavior or NSSI (Linehan, 2000). In addition, because individuals who engage in NSSI do not express or exhibit the intent to die, they are unlikely to be admitted to hospitals unless they have serious injuries. As a result, hospitalization as a form of treatment for self-injury is now used less frequently than in the past, leaving mental health professionals, including those working in schools, with greater treatment responsibilities (Muehlenkamp, 2006).

Unfortunately, there is little empirical data available that could be used to guide the psychosocial treatment of individuals exhibiting NSSI. Because of ethical, legal, and logistical issues, few large-scale treatment studies include self-injuring or suicidal individuals (Linehan, 2000), and very few studies specifically target NSSI behaviors as the main focus on treatment (Muehlenkamp, 2006). Further, most of the published treatment studies have been conducted with adults rather than children or adolescents. Consequently, much more research regarding psychosocial interventions for NSSI needs to be completed before more definitive conclusions regarding their effectiveness can be made (Nixon, Aulakh, Townsend, & Atherton, 2009).

However, as noted by Muehlenkamp (2006) in her review of empirically supported treatments for NSSI, "given that non-suicidal self-injury is primarily conceptualized as a tool for emotion regulation maintained through positive and negative reinforcements, treatments utilizing cognitive-behavioral strategies show the greatest promise for successfully reducing the behavior" (p. 167). Cognitive-behavioral interventions have demonstrated effectiveness at reducing repetitive suicidal behaviors (Evans, 2000) and related conditions such as depression in both youth (Merrell, 2008a) and adults (Beck et al., 1979). First described in the 1950s and 1960s, cognitive-behavior therapy (CBT) derived primarily from social learning theory and cognitive psychology, and may be best described as a general therapy category rather than a distinct technique (Nixon et al., 2009). Several approaches to CBT have been proposed, the most prominent of which have been Ellis' rational-emotive therapy (Ellis, 1962), Beck's cognitive therapy (Beck et al., 1979), and Meichenbaum's cognitive-behavior modification (Meichenbaum, 1977). CBT is one of the most well-researched and effective treatments for a variety of psychological disorders in children, adolescents, and adults, and has demonstrated particular utility in the treatment of internalizing disorders such as depression and anxiety.

Nixon and colleagues (2009) describe the common principles of cognitive-behavior therapies as follows:

- Cognition, not external factors, both mediate and cause one's feelings and overt behaviors, allowing clients to change their maladaptive behaviors to feel and behave more adaptively, even if little in the environment around them changes.
- Client beliefs are primarily the result of learning experiences and thus can be changed; the goal of treatment is often to unlearn related maladaptive feelings and behaviors by identifying those that are irrational and generating more rational alternative beliefs.
- More emphasis should be put on the here and now and situationally specific beliefs and behaviors rather than general or stable personality traits.
- The essence of effective therapy is to assist clients in developing more awareness of the role their irrational beliefs play in distress and helping them change those beliefs. CBT recognizes that these irrational beliefs are more common among persons with anxiety, depression, and so on and are based upon errors in reasoning or logic. (p. 227)

Other characteristics of CBT include the following:

- It is highly structured, systematic, time-limited intervention in which the therapist plays an active role.
- Although a strong therapeutic alliance is essential for CBT, it is not considered sufficient for effective treatment to occur.
- CBT makes use of the Socratic method in therapy, to assist and challenge clients to question their often hidden, underlying, and irrational assumptions, beliefs, and thoughts.
- CBT incorporates both cognitive strategies designed to modify thoughts and behavioral strategies (e.g., activity scheduling, exposure) designed to modify environments; both are considered essential elements of CBT.
- "Homework" is essential in CBT; clients are expected to apply and practice in real situations what they learn and discuss in therapy sessions.

Students who engage in NSSI, and whose triggers for it may be associated with significant symptoms of depression and/or anxiety, as well as those exhibiting irrational thought processes and a host of maladaptive behaviors, may be best suited to CBT as an initial intervention (Nixon et al., 2009). In her comprehensive literature review of interventions for NSSI, Muehlenkamp (2006) identified two psychosocial treatments as having the most empirical support for their effectiveness, both of which can be categorized as cognitive-behavioral: problem-solving therapy and dialectical behavior therapy. In the discussion that follows, particular emphasis is given to reviewing dialectical behavior therapy, as this therapeutic approach currently appears to have the most empirical support for its treatment effectiveness in the professional literature.

Problem-Solving Therapy

The major assumption underlying the use of Problem-Solving Therapy (PST) is that dysfunctional coping behaviors occur as a result of cognitive or behavioral breakdowns in the problem-solving process (D'Zurilla & Nezu, 2001). Although PST was not developed specifically to treat NSSI, it has been used to treat it as well as a number of other psychological problems. In describing PST, Muehlenkamp (2006) states that the goal of therapy is:

> ... to help clients identify and resolve the problems they encounter in their lives, as well as to teach clients general coping and problem-solving skills that they can utilize in the future to deal more effectively with the problems they encounter. This is usually done by teaching the different steps in problem solving including problem identification and goal setting (often by utilizing a behavioral analysis of the problem), brainstorming and assessing potential solutions, selecting and implementing a solution, and evaluating the success of the chosen solution. (p. 168)

Teaching these steps is considered important in reducing NSSI, as research has consistently found that individuals who engage in self-injury frequently exhibit poor problem-solving skills (Pollock & Williams, 1998; Speckens & Hawton, 2005) and tend to have rigid styles of thinking (Kernberg, 1994). PST also stresses the importance of forming a strong, therapeutic relationship with the client, so that the teaching of skills and putting them into practice becomes a collaborative process (Muehlenkamp, 2006).

Research on the efficacy of PST in reducing self-injury has yielded mixed results, making it difficult to draw specific conclusions (Muehlenkamp, 2006). Further, although a few studies have emerged suggesting that PST has the potential to significantly reduce NSSI, Muehlenkamp (2006) concluded that the PSTs that demonstrated the most promise for long-term efficacy in reducing NSSI were those that incorporated "additional cognitive, interpersonal, or behavioral elements into the standard problem-solving protocol, suggesting that a comprehensive approach may be best" (p. 169). Moreover, these studies have generally been conducted with adults rather than children or adolescents, making it even more difficult to form conclusions about the effectiveness of PST for reducing NSSI in school-age populations. However, this treatment approach does appear to have the potential to be effective with youth engaging in NSSI, especially when combined with other cognitive-behavioral strategies, although more research evaluating it in this context is clearly needed.

Dialectical Behavior Therapy

Dialectical behavior therapy (DBT) is a cognitive-behavioral treatment for complex, difficult to treat mental health disorders and problems. Dimeff and Linehan (2001) provide the following description:

> DBT combines the basic strategies of behavior therapy with eastern mindfulness practices, residing within an overarching dialectical worldview that emphasizes the synthesis of opposites. The term dialectical is also meant to convey both the multiple tensions that co-occur in therapy with suicidal clients with [borderline personality disorder] as well as the emphasis in DBT on enhancing dialectical thinking patterns to replace rigid, dichotomous thinking. The fundamental dialectic in DBT is between validation and acceptance of the client as they are within the context of simultaneously helping them to change. Acceptance procedures in DBT include mindfulness (e.g., attention to the present moment, assuming a nonjudgmental stance, focusing on effectiveness) and a variety of validation and acceptance-based stylistic strategies. Change strategies in DBT include behavioral analysis of maladaptive behaviors and problem-solving techniques, including skills training, contingency management (i.e., reinforcers, punishment), cognitive modification, and exposure-based strategies. (p. 10)

Like other so-called "third-wave" behavior therapies ("first-wave" behavior therapies emphasized the application of basic behavioral principles to clinical problems; "second-wave" behavior therapies added a cognitive component via the elimination or replacement of irrational, problematic thoughts; O'Brien, Larson, & Murrell, 2008) such as Acceptance and Commitment Therapy (ACT; Hayes, Strosahl, & Wilson, 1999), Functional Analytic Psychotherapy (FAP; Kohlenberg & Tsai, 1991), and Mindfulness-Based Cognitive Therapy (MBCT;

Segal, Williams, & Teasdale, 2002), DBT emphasizes two fundamental and related concepts: *acceptance* and *mindfulness* (Greco & Hayes, 2008; Hayes, Follette, & Linehan, 2004).

Acceptance. DBT and other third-wave therapies focus on both acceptance of problems *and* changing them – ideas which would perhaps initially appear to be both polar opposites and mutually exclusive. However, as noted by O'Brien and colleagues (2008):

> The goal of these techniques is not to change problematic thoughts or emotions, but rather to accept them for what they are – just private experiences, not literal truth. In this view, acceptance is accompanied by change, but the change is of a different sort than that seen in traditional cognitive-behavioral therapies: rather than changing the content of their thoughts, clients are changing their relationship to their thoughts. The careful balance of acceptance and change, referred to as the central dialectic in DBT, characterizes a dialectic common to all third-wave therapies. When clients are able to balance acceptance and change, accepting their thoughts as thoughts and thereby changing their relationship to their thoughts, they gain the flexibility to move in valued directions. (p. 16)

DBT therefore differs from traditional cognitive-behavior therapies in its treatment of private events and internal experiences, such as thoughts, feelings, and bodily/physical sensations. As noted by Hayes and Greco (2008): "Rather than targeting and attempting to change the content, frequency, and form of thoughts and feelings directly, acceptance-based approaches. . .seek to alter the function of internal phenomena so as to diminish their behavioral impact" (p. 3). As such, professionals who are familiar and comfortable with traditional cognitive-behavioral techniques, particularly those that emphasize cognitive restructuring and the disputation of irrational thoughts and beliefs, may initially find the "mental shift" necessary to understand third-wave approaches (such as DBT) difficult, given that these techniques are so different from the basic premises of cognitive therapy (Merrell, 2008a). In particular, in contrast to the emphasis in traditional cognitive-behavior therapy on changing the *contents* of the client's thoughts, DBT emphasizes changing the client's *relationship* to their thoughts (O'Brien et al., 2008).

Mindfulness. In addition to embracing acceptance, another common element in third-wave behavior therapies such as DBT is their emphasis on *mindfulness*. Mindfulness is "paying attention in a particular way; on purpose, in the present moment, and nonjudgmentally" (Kabat-Zinn, 1994, p. 4). Defined in this way, mindfulness would necessarily entail being present and nonjudgmental even in those situations and moments that are most unpleasant and painful (O'Brien et al., 2008). Engaging in mindfulness requires three different but interrelated elements: observing, describing, and participating. More specifically, "observing entails watching one's own thoughts, feelings, and behaviors without trying to change them; describing refers to the labeling of thoughts, feelings, and behaviors without judgment; and participating requires complete involvement in the present moment, without self-consciousness" (O'Brien et al., 2008, p. 21). Although the application of mindfulness procedures for addressing mental health problems has a relatively recent history (Greco & Hayes, 2008), the practice of mindfulness has been practiced by Buddhists for over 2,500 years (Kabat-Zinn, 2003).

Mindfulness-based interventions with youth are gaining increasing attention in the professional literature, particularly for their potential utility in the treatment of child and adolescent internalizing disorders and problems (e.g., Greco & Hayes, 2008; Merrell, 2008a; Miller & Nickerson, 2007b; Miller et al., 2009), including self-injury (Wagner, Rathus, & Miller, 2006). Indeed, mindfulness and youth would appear to be logically and naturally related. For example, within Buddhism, the concept of "beginner's mind" refers to particular qualities of mindfulness, including being open, receptive, and willing and ready to learn (Goodman, 2005; Kabat-Zinn, 1990); these qualities often better characterize the young rather than older adults, who are often more set in their ways. As noted by O'Brien and colleagues (2008):

> Beginners are more enthusiastic and less cynical about learning; they possess a curiosity that adults seem to have lost and are more receptive to new ideas and experiences. Compared to adults, youth are beginners in life's journey, and the therapist who adopts a beginner's mind gains a window into the mind of the child as beginner and can better enter into the child's world. As such, acceptance and mindfulness practices seem particularly suited to working with youth. (p. 17)

DBT and the Treatment of Self-Injury

Originally developed by Linehan (1993), DBT grew out of a series of failed attempts to apply standard cognitive-behavior therapy protocols to chronically suicidal adult clients with comorbid borderline personality disorder (Dimeff & Linehan, 2001). It has since been adapted for a variety of other problems involving emotion dysregulation, such as substance abuse and binge eating (Dimeff & Linehan, 2001), and has emerged as a potentially useful treatment for NSSI (Klonsky & Muehlenkamp, 2007). Moreover, in recent years DBT has been used successfully to treat child and adolescent populations (e.g., Callahan, 2008; Woodberry, Roy, & Indik, 2008), including adolescents exhibiting suicidal behavior (Miller, Rathus, & Linehan, 2007) and self-injury (Nock, Teper, & Hollander, 2007).

As noted above, the core dialectic in standard DBT is the balance between acceptance and change (Linehan, 1993). Because DBT was largely developed and implemented initially with adults with borderline personality disorder who exhibited the combination of a biological predisposition toward emotional dysregulation and an invalidating social environment (Linehan, 1993), DBT therapists attempt to provide validation of their clients through acceptance. Under this framework, acceptance refers to "the ability to view previously unacceptable thoughts, emotions, and behaviors as valid given a particular context" (O'Brien et al., 2008, p. 20).

Mindfulness is one of the core skills taught to individuals struggling with this seeming polarity of acceptance and change. Although mindfulness is not the only skill taught in DBT, the teaching and practice of mindfulness provides a base from which other needed skills can be developed, including skills in distress tolerance, emotion regulation, and interpersonal effectiveness (Wagner et al., 2006). As noted by O'Brien and colleagues (2008):

By cultivating a nonjudgmental awareness of the present moment, individuals...can better observe and label their emotions without impulsively acting on them; their tolerance for distressing feelings thereby increases, their ability to regulate emotions improves, and they can thus more effectively relate to others, whose emotions are also observed and labeled nonjudgmentally. (p. 20)

Nock et al. (2007) describe the role and function of the DBT therapist as follows:

1. The DBT clinician carefully identifies and operationalizes the target behaviors to be changed in treatment (using a comprehensive assessment of mental disorders, problem behaviors, and client functioning) and continuously measures these over the course of treatment.
2. The DBT clinician helps the client to identify the antecedents and consequences of their self-injury and other target behaviors so that they will better understand their behaviors and will be able to modify them.
3. Once the clinician and client understand the functions of the client's self-injury, they work together to develop other alternative and incompatible behaviors to replace it.
4. As with other forms of behavior therapy, the clinician attempts to modify the client's environment to achieve behavior change, and with adolescents this involves working with the (student's) family throughout the course of treatment.
5. In addition to sharing the treatment philosophy and plan with the family, the clinician works to modify their interactions with the adolescent when necessary, such as by teaching parent management skills. (p. 1084)

DBT therapists working with students who exhibit NSSI should first work with students to commit to treatment and then focus on the main targets of DBT, which include (a) decreasing life-threatening behaviors; (b) decreasing therapy-interfering behaviors; (c) decreasing quality of life-interfering behaviors, and (d) increasing behavioral skills. The main skills taught to students during DBT therapy sessions should include mindfulness, emotional regulation, interpersonal effectiveness, distress tolerance, and "walking the middle path" skills (Nock et al., 2007). This last skill module is a unique aspect of adolescent DBT, and involves teaching several family-focused skills including validation of self and others, the use of behavioral principles, and common adolescent–family dilemmas (Nock et al., 2007). Although DBT therapy for adults is recommended to occur for at least 1 year, an outpatient version of DBT for adolescents developed by Miller and colleagues (2007) is significantly shorter and can be completed within a 16-week period.

A more comprehensive discussion of DBT is beyond the scope of this book. School-based mental health practitioners interested in more information on this topic, including its practical applications, are encouraged to review other sources, including Linehan (1993), Callahan (2008), and especially Miller and colleagues (2007). Readers interested in more information on psychosocial treatment approaches for NSSI in general, including DBT, are encouraged to review Walsh (2006), D'Onofrio (2007), and Nixon and Heath (2009b).

The Psychopharmacological Treatment of NSSI

School-based professionals who are involved, either directly or indirectly, with treating students with NSSI should be aware of pertinent issues in the psychopharmacological treatment of self-injury. Unfortunately, although there is research available documenting the effectiveness of psychopharmacological interventions for reducing some of the mental disorders commonly associated with self-injury, such as depression and anxiety (e.g., Bridge et al., 2007) and borderline personality disorder (e.g., Nose, Cipriani, & Biancosino, 2006), the authors are, to date, not aware of any studies that have evaluated the effectiveness of different medications in reducing NSSI (Klonsky & Muehlenkamp, 2007). Moreover, most of the studies that have examined the effects of medication on mental health disorders related to NSSI have been conducted with adults rather than children or adolescents, although there is growing support for the efficacy of antidepressant medication for the treatment of depression in children and adolescents (Noggle & Dean, 2009). Consequently, the reader should be aware that the knowledge base regarding psychopharmacological interventions for the treatment of NSSI is currently quite limited. In fact, no medication has been currently approved as demonstrating clear effectiveness in treating NSSI specifically (Plener, Libal, & Nixon, 2009).

Nevertheless, psychopharmacological interventions for students engaging in NSSI should be seriously considered if (a) the student is exhibiting a comorbid psychiatric disorder with sufficient evidence of the effectiveness of medication for its treatment, such as depression, and (b) the student is not sufficiently responsive to psychosocial interventions (Plener et al., 2009). If medications are prescribed by medical professionals, appropriate school personnel (e.g., school nurses) can assist teachers and other school staff members in monitoring medication effects in schools, and there is evidence to suggest that this is a role they are willing and able to perform (e.g., Gureasko-Moore, DuPaul, & Power, 2005). However, for this to occur school personnel will need to be adequately trained (Pierson, 2009a) to be cognizant of appropriate ethical and legal issues regarding medications in schools (Mazar-Mosiewicz, Pierson, & McIntosh, 2009); able to work collaboratively with other school personnel (Anderson, Walcott, Reck, & Landau, 2009); able to effectively evaluate the effects of medication (Riley-Tillman & Burns, 2009); and able to develop, implement, and sustain agile, flexible medication monitoring systems (Volpe, Heick, & Gureasko-Moore, 2005) that are feasible, acceptable, and perceived to be effective (Anderson et al., 2009).

In general, medications for NSSI should be used as an ancillary, adjunctive intervention to ongoing psychosocial treatments and can be potentially useful in augmenting their effects. For example, antidepressant medication might be administered to a student who exhibits depression as well as NSSI, and may be useful in enhancing the student's mood and motivation to receive psychosocial treatment for both problems (Plener et al., 2009). The example of antidepressants is an especially pertinent one, given that NSSI is highly associated with both suicide and mood disorders, and these latter two conditions are frequently treated with antidepressant medication. Consequently, it is particularly important that school personnel be aware of the effectiveness of antidepressant medication for internalizing problems in children and youth.

Medications described as "antidepressants" are generally classified into one of four groups: monoamine oxidase inhibitors (MAOIs), tricyclic antidepressants (TCAs), selective serotonin reuptake inhibitors (SSRIs), and selective norepinephrine reuptake inhibitors (SNRIs). The four groups are each described as antidepressants because of their impact; however, as noted by Noggle and Dean (2009), "they differ substantially in their chemical makeup, which corresponds with discrepancies in clinical indications, efficacy, and adverse effects" (p. 859). Moreover, although the professional literature suggests that antidepressant medications are not typically used until other, non-psychopharmacological treatment options have been explored and exhausted (Garland, 2004), it is clear that the use of these types of medications have increased substantially and become a central form of treatment for children and youth (Wong, Besag, Santosh, & Murray, 2004). In recent years, the use of antidepressants with children and youth has become highly controversial because of proposed links between their use and suicidal behavior.

Antidepressant Medication and Suicidality

The controversy regarding the use of antidepressant medication with pediatric populations began when research suggested that paroxetine (Paxil), an SSRI, was found to produce a slight increase in suicidal ideation and behavior in children and adolescents with major depressive disorder. This led to public concerns voiced by the Food and Drug Administration (FDA) as well as other regulatory agencies concerned with health, safety, and consumer protection (Kratochvil et al., 2006). In 2004, the results of a meta-analysis involving 24 controlled clinical trials (involving approximately 4,400 pediatric patients) of nine antidepressant medications were presented at a public hearing. The reported results indicated no suicides within any of the trials, and the cumulative risk of spontaneously reported suicidal ideation was 4% for active medication and 2% for placebo (Hammad, Laughren, & Racoosin, 2006). Following this hearing and recommendations from various public health and psychopharmacological organizations, in late 2004 the FDA issued its "black-box" warning for all antidepressants, which suggested that an increased risk of suicidality may accompany the use of antidepressants with pediatric populations (Hammad et al., 2006).

After this warning was publicly announced, and presumably in large part because of it, the number of antidepressant prescriptions written for pediatric populations decreased significantly (Bhatia et al., 2008). Similarly, the number of child and adolescent cases of depression as diagnosed by physicians has decreased as well (Libby et al., 2007). Prior to the FDA's "black-box" warnings, approximately 20% of antidepressant medications went unfilled; by October of 2005 (1 year after the warnings), that figure had risen to more than 60% (Pierson, 2009b).

Ironically, there is now speculation that the decreased numbers of youth taking antidepressant medication as a result of fears about its possible relationship to suicidality may be at least partly responsible for a recent *increase* in youth suicide (Gibbons et al., 2007). In a recent review, Bostwick (2006) found the evidence for a relationship between youth suicide and antidepressants to be "underwhelming" and suggested that, if vulnerability to suicide from medication exists, it is more likely to develop in the first few weeks after beginning medication, and that the more time an individual is medicated the less likely suicidal behavior will occur. Similarly, Pierson (2009b) concluded that although "individuals do have an increased risk of suicidal ideation when being treated with a limited number of SSRIs...the increased risk of suicidal ideation has not been shown to lead to an increased rate of suicidal behavior or completion over the rates seen in the general population" (p. 913). Further, there is evidence to suggest that the increased risk of suicidal ideation seen in some youth may not be the result of medication but may rather be an artifact of other variables (Pierson, 2009b).

Clearly, although evidence suggests that sometimes *not* prescribing antidepressant medication may be more harmful than administering it to students, school personnel should be proactive in the monitoring of possible suicidal ideation in youth with comorbid NSSI and depression receiving antidepressants (Pierson, 2009b). For more information on the topic of psychopharmacological interventions for students with NSSI, the reader is encouraged to review Plener and colleagues (2009).

Recommendations for Schools

It is important that school-based mental health professionals be able to identify youth who self-injure; correctly differentiate self-injury from suicide attempts; and respond quickly, appropriately, and effectively to instances of NSSI when they occur. In doing so, school personnel should practice within the boundaries of their training and competence, and collaborate effectively with professionals both in the school and outside of it to ensure that students engaging in NSSI receive the best possible treatment. Kanan and colleagues (2008) provide the following recommendations for school personnel and their role in identifying, assessing, and treating self-injury:

- Provide awareness and knowledge to school personnel about NSSI
- Educate students about the need to report any instances of NSSI, whether they directly observe it or simply suspect it
- Use a team approach to responding to students engaging in NSSI
- Provide appropriate support for students engaging in NSSI
- Screen students for NSSI as well as possible comorbid disorders and suicide risk
- Notify and provide resources to parents/caregivers of students engaging in NSSI
- Develop short-term plans for safety of students engaging in NSSI

- Collaborate with treatment providers in the community in working with students engaging in NSSI
- Effectively manage any possible contagion effects

Concluding Comments

The treatment of NSSI is a complex process, but one in which school personnel play an important role. A school-based, public health approach to the prevention and treatment of NSSI was presented, along with guidelines and recommendations for effectively responding to NSSI when it occurs, including suggestions for responding to possible contagion effects. Psychosocial interventions for NSSI were discussed, including a particular emphasis on the potential utility of dialectical behavior therapy in this process. Psychopharmacological interventions that may be useful in the treatment of NSSI were also reviewed, particularly the use of antidepressant medication and the controversy over its use. Finally, summary recommendations were provided regarding the roles and responsibilities of school personnel when confronted by students exhibiting NSSI. It is our hope that this chapter, as well as this book as a whole, will be a helpful and practical resource to school-based practitioners attempting to better identify, assess, and treat self-injury at school.

Appendix
Self-Injury Internet Resources

Although some Web sites on the Internet are counterproductive because they encourage and incite individuals to engage in self-injury, rather than provide assistance and support to reduce or eliminate it, there are other sites that provide useful information for school personnel, mental health practitioners, and parents or caregivers (as well as for individuals who self-injure). However, the vast amount of information that can be retrieved in any given Internet search can make this an effortful, time-consuming, and sometimes overwhelming task. Some useful Web sites devoted to NSSI and related topics are listed below. Some of these Web sites are designed by mental health professionals; others were created by self-injurers offering peer support and advice. All can be potentially useful to school personnel interested in learning more about self-injury, or as sources of information, assistance, and support to youth engaging in NSSI. The list is by no means comprehensive or exhaustive, but it does contain links to some of the Web-based materials and information that the authors suggest may be helpful.

American Self-Harm Information Clearing House

www.selfinjury.org

The American Self-Harm Information Clearinghouse (ASHIC) has the stated goal of increasing public awareness of the phenomenon of self-inflicted violence and the challenges faced by self-injurers and their caregivers. The ASHIC Web page states, "The first step toward coping with self-injurious behavior is education: bringing reliable information about who self-injures, why they do it, and how they can learn to stop to people who self-injure and to their friends, loved ones, and medical caregivers. ASHIC was founded to meet this need for honest, accurate information." Its Web page includes a definition of self-injury and well as a discussion of common myths about these behaviors.

D.N. Miller, S.E. Brock, *Identifying, Assessing, and Treating Self-Injury at School*,
Developmental Psychopathology at School, DOI 10.1007/978-1-4419-6092-4,
© Springer Science+Business Media, LLC 2010

BUS (Bodies Under Siege) Central

www.buslist.org

This Web page provides downloadable audio files examining the topic of self-injury. In addition it offers a list of what it identifies as "good articles" suggested to provide helpful information on this topic.

Life SIGNS: Self-Injury Guidance and Network Support

www.lifesigns.org.uk

Based in the United Kingdom, this Web page strives to raise awareness about self-injury and to help people who rely on these behaviors. It strives to do so by "providing a safe, friendly message board, ideas for distraction techniques and by inspiring/empowering them to find alternative, healthier coping mechanisms." Its resources include "What SI is," Helping you," "Guidance for Others," "Professionals," "Coming Out," "Message Board," "Publications," and "Newsletter." The Professionals sections provides articles and resources, as well as a message board for professionals.

RecoverYourLife.com

www.recoveryourlife.com

Based in the United Kingdom, this Web site provides direct support to individuals who self-injure, including articles and 24/7 assistance and support. It offers a variety of "distraction" behaviors, which provide alternatives to self-injury behaviors.

S.A.F.E. (Self-Abuse Finally Ends) Alternatives

www.selfinjury.com

S.A.F.E. Alternatives® is the Web site for a treatment program that also offers a professional network and educational resources (including a listing of journal articles and books). Treatment referral resources are also offered.

Self-Injury: You are NOT the only one

www.selfharm.net

This evolving Web page includes links that provides basic descriptive information about self-injury and immediate and long-term treatment options. References and offline resources are also offered. Resources for friends and family members of those who self-injure are provided.

Self-Injury: Support

www.sisupport.org

This site has as its stated mission "To offer a positive and productive self-injury support site providing alternatives to self-injury, referrals, support groups, affirmations and interactive opportunities." It includes resources to facilitate recovery and obtain professional help.

SIARI (Self-Injury and Related Issues)

www.siari.co.uk

Based in the United Kingdom, this Web site strives to increase self-injury awareness and aims and providing coping resources. It includes guidance for self-injurers as well as for their families and friends, and for professionals.

References

Achenbach, T. M. (2001). *Child behavior checklist for ages 6–18.* Burlington, VT: Research Center for Children, Youth, and Families.

Alderman, T. (1997). *Scarred soul: Understanding and ending self-inflicted violence.* Oakland, CA: New Harbinger.

Alexander, L. A. (1999). The functions of self-injury and its link to traumatic events in college students. *UMI ProQuest Digital Dissertations,* 24. (preview, 9932285).

Allen Heath, M., & Sheen, D. (2005). *School-based crisis intervention: Preparing all personnel to assist.* New York: Guilford Press.

American Psychiatric Association. (2000). *Diagnostic and statistical manual of mental disorders* (4th ed., text rev.). Washington, DC: Author.

Anderson, L., Walcott, C. M., Reck, S. G., & Landau, S. (2009). Issues in monitoring medication effects in the classroom. *Psychology in the Schools, 46,* 820–826.

Andover, M. S., Pepper, C. M., Ryabchenko, K. A., Orrico, E. G., & Gibb. B. E. (2005). Self-mutilation and symptoms of depression, anxiety, and borderline personality disorder. *Suicide and Life-Threatening Behavior, 35,* 581–591.

Appleton, J. J., Christenson, S. L., & Furlong, M. J. (2008). Student engagement with school: Critical conceptual and methodological issues of the construct. *Psychology in the Schools, 45,* 369–386.

Bardos, A. N. (1993). Human figure drawings: Abusing the abused. *School Psychology Quarterly, 8,* 177–181.

Batsche, G. M., & Peterson, D. W. (1983). School psychology and projective assessment: A growing incompatibility. *School Psychology Review, 12,* 440–445.

Bearman, P., & Moody, J. (2004). Suicide and friendships among American adolescents. *American Journal of Public Health, 94,* 89–95.

Beck, A. T. (1976). *Cognitive therapy and the emotional disorders.* New York: New American Library.

Beck, A. T., Rush, A. J., Shaw, B. F., & Emery, G. (1979). *Cognitive therapy of depression.* New York: Guilford Press.

Beck, J. S. (1995). *Cognitive therapy: Basics and beyond.* New York: Guilford Press.

Berman, A. L. (2009). School-based suicide prevention: Research advances and practice implications. *School Psychology Review, 38,* 233–238.

Berman, A. L., Jobes, D. A., & Silverman, M. M. (2006). *Adolescent suicide: Assessment and intervention* (2nd ed.). Washington, DC: American Psychological Association.

Bersoff, D. N., & Koeppl, P. M. (1993). The relation between ethical codes and moral principles. *Ethics and Behavior, 3,* 345–357.

Bhatia, S. K., Rezak, A. J., Vitello, B., Sitorius, M. A., Buehler, B. A., & Kratochvil, C. J. (2008). Antidepressant prescribing practices for the treatment of children and adolescents. *Journal of Child and Adolescent Psychopharmacology, 18,* 70–80.

Boman, P., Furlong, M. J., Shochet, I., Lilles, E., & Jones, C. (2009). Optimism and the school context. In R. Gilman, E. S. Huebner, & M. J. Furlong (Eds.), *Handbook of positive psychology in schools* (pp. 51–64). New York: Routledge.

Bostwick, J. M. (2006). Do SSRIs cause suicide in children? The evidence is underwhelming. *Journal of Clinical Psychology, 62*, 235–241.

Bowman, S., & Randall, K. (2006). *See my pain! Creative strategies and activities for helping young people who self-injure.* Chapin, SC: YouthLight, Inc.

Bridge, J. A., Iyengar, S., Salary, C. B., Barbe, R. P., Birmaher, B., Pincus, H. A., et al. (2007). Clinical response and risk for reported suicidal ideation and suicide attempts in pediatric antide-pressant treatment: A meta-analysis of randomized controlled trials. *Journal of the American Medical Association, 297*, 1683–1696.

Briere, J., & Gil, E. (1998). Self-mutilation in clinical and general population samples: Prevalence, correlates, and functions. *American Journal of Orthopsychiatry, 64*, 609–620.

Brock, S. E. (2002a). Estimating the appropriate crisis response. In S. E. Brock, P. J. Lazarus, & S. R. Jimerson (Eds.), *Best practices in school crisis prevention and intervention* (pp. 355–366). Bethesda, MD: National Association of School Psychologists.

Brock, S. E. (2002b). Identifying individuals at risk for psychological trauma. In S. E. Brock, P. J. Lazarus, & S. R. Jimerson (Eds.), *Best practices in school crisis prevention and intervention* (pp. 367–384). Bethesda, MD: National Association of School Psychologists.

Brock, S. E. (2006). *Crisis intervention and recovery: The roles of school-based mental health professionals.* Bethesda, MD: National Association of School Psychologists.

Brock, S. E., & Clinton, A. (2007). Diagnosis of attention-deficit/hyperactivity disorder (AD/HD) in childhood: A review of the literature. *The California School Psychologist, 12*, 73–91.

Brock, S. E., Jimerson, S. R., & Hansen, R. L. (2006). *Identifying, assessing, and treating autism at school.* New York: Springer.

Brock, S. E., Lazarus, P. J., & Jimerson, S. R. (Eds.). (2002). *Best practices in school crisis prevention and intervention.* Bethesda, MD: National Association of School Psychologists.

Brock, S. E., Nickerson, A. B., Reeves, M. A., & Jimerson, S. R. (2008). Best practices for school psychologists as members of crisis teams: The PREPaRe model. In A. Thomas & J. Grimes (Eds.), *Best practices in school psychology V* (Vol. 5, pp. 1487–1504). Bethesda, MD: National Association of School Psychologists.

Brock, S. E., Nickerson, A. B., Reeves, M. A., Jimerson, S. R., Lieberman, R., & Feinberg, T. (2008). *School crisis prevention and intervention: The PREPaRE model.* Bethesda, MD: National Association of School Psychologists.

Brock, S. E., Sandoval, J., & Hart, S. (2006). Suicidal ideation and behaviors. In G. C. Bear, K. M. Minke, & A. Thomas (Eds.), *Children's needs III: Development, prevention and intervention* (pp. 225–238). Bethesda, MD: National Association of School Psychologists.

Brock, S. E., Sandoval, J., & Lewis, S. (2001). *Preparing for crises in the schools: A manual for building school crisis response teams* (2nd ed.). New York: Wiley.

Brown, L. S., & Bryan, T. C. (2007). Feminist therapy with people who self-inflict violence. *Journal of Clinical Psychology: In Session, 63*, 1121–1133.

Brown, M. Z., Comtois, K. A., & Linehan, M. M. (2002). Reasons for suicide attempts and non-suicidal self-injury in women with borderline personality disorder. *Journal of Abnormal Psychology, 111*, 198–202.

Buckley, M., & Saarni, C. (2009). Emotion regulation. In R. Gilman, E. S. Huebner, & M. J. Furlong (Eds.), *Handbook of positive psychology in schools* (pp. 107–118). New York: Routledge.

Burns, M. K., & Klingbeil, D. A. (2010). Assessment of academic skills in math within a problem-solving model. In G. Gimpel Peacock, R. A. Ervin, E. J. Daly, & K. W. Merrell (Eds.), *Practical handbook of school psychology: Effective practices for the 21st century* (pp. 86–98). New York: Guilford Press.

Burrow-Sanchez, J. J., & Hawken, L. S. (2007). *Helping students overcome substance abuse: Effective practices for prevention and intervention.* New York: Guilford Press.

Callahan, C. (2008). *Dialectical behavior therapy: Children and adolescents.* Eau Claire, WI: Pesi.

Carlson, M. (2005). *Blade silver: Color me scarred.* London: Think Books.

Carney, M. (2005). *Stitched: A memoir.* Frederick, MD: PublishAmerica.

Caron, C., & Rutter, M. (1991). Comorbidity in child psychopathology: Concepts, issues, and research strategies. *Journal of Child Psychology and Psychiatry and Allied Disciplines, 32,* 1063–1080.

Chandler, L. A. (2003). The projective hypothesis and the development of projective techniques for children. In C. R. Reynolds & R. W. Kamphaus (Eds.), *Handbook of psychological and educational assessment of children: Personality, behavior, and context* (pp. 51–65). New York: Guilford Press.

Cicchetti, D., & Toth, S. L. (2005). Child maltreatment. *Annual Review of Clinical Psychology, 1,* 409–438.

Claes, L., & Vandereycken, W. (2007). Self-injurious behavior: Differential diagnosis and functional differentiation. *Comprehensive Psychiatry, 48,* 137–144.

Clarke, A. (1999). *Coping with self-mutilation: A helping book for teens who hurt themselves.* New York: Rosen Publishing Group.

Cleveland Clinic. (2009). Self-injury. http://my.clevelandclinic.org/disorders/self-injury/hic_self-injury.aspx. Retrieved 7 September 2009.

Cloutier, P., & Humphreys, L. (2009). Measurement of nonsuicidal self-injury in adolescents. In M. K. Nixon & N. L. Heath (Eds.), *Self-injury in youth: The essential guide to assessment and intervention* (pp. 115–142). New York: Routledge.

Connors, R. E. (2000). *Self-injury: Psychotherapy with people who engage in self-inflicted violence.* Northvale, NJ: Jason Aronson.

Conterio, K., & Lader, W. (1998). *Bodily harm: The breakthrough healing program for self injurers.* New York: Hyperion Press.

Crouch, W., & Wright, J. (2004). Deliberate self-harm in an adolescent unit: A qualitative investigation. *Clinical Child Psychology & Psychiatry, 9,* 185–204.

Crowell, S. E., Beauchaine, T. P., Smith, C. J., Vasilev, C. A., & Stevens, A. L. (2008). Parent-child interactions, peripheral serotonin, and self-inflicted injury in adolescents. *Journal of Consulting and Clinical Psychology, 76,* 15–21.

Davis, J. M., & Sandoval, J. (1991). *Suicidal youth: School-based intervention and prevention.* San Francisco, CA: Jossey-Bass.

Dawes, R. M. (1994). *House of cards: Psychology and psychotherapy built on myth.* New York: Free Press.

DeLeo, D., & Heller, T. S. (2004). Who are the kids who self-harm? An Australian self-report school survey. *Medical Journal of Australia, 181,* 140–144.

Demaray, M. K., & Malecki, C. K. (2002). The relationship between perceived social support and maladjustment for students at risk. *Psychology in the Schools, 39,* 305–316.

Dieter, P. J., Nicholls, S. S., & Pearlman, L. A. (2000). Self-injury and self-capacities: Assisting an individual in crisis. *Journal of Clinical Psychology, 56,* 1173–1191.

Dimeff, L., & Linehan, M. M. (2001). Dialectical behavior therapy in a nutshell. *The California Psychologist, 34,* 10–13.

Doll, B., & Cummings, J. A. (Eds.). (2008). *Transforming school mental health services.* Thousand Oaks, CA: Corwin Press.

D'Onofrio, A. A. (2007). *Adolescent self injury: A comprehensive guide for counselors and health care professionals.* New York: Springer.

Dowdy, E., Mays, K. L., Kamphaus, R. W., & Reynolds, C. R. (2009). Roles of diagnosis and classification in school psychology. In T. B. Gutkin & C. R. Reynolds (Eds.), *The handbook of school psychology* (4th ed., pp. 191–209). New York: Wiley.

D'Zurilla, T. J., & Nezu, A. M. (2001). Problem solving therapies. In K. Dobson (Ed.), *Handbook of cognitive-behavioral therapies* (2nd ed., pp. 211–245). New York: Guilford Press.

Eckert, T. L., Dunn, E. K., Guiney, K. M., & Codding, R. S. (2000). Self-reports: Theory and research in using rating scale measures. In E. S. Shapiro & T. R. Krachochwill (Eds.),

Behavioral assessment in schools: Theory, research, and clinical foundations (2nd ed., pp. 288–322). New York: Guilford Press.

Ellis, A. (1962). *Reason and emotion in psychotherapy.* New York: Lyle Stewart.

Engstrom, K., Diderichsen, R., & Laflamme, L. (2004). Parental social determinants of risk for intentional injury: A cross-sectional study of Swedish adolescents. *American Journal of Public Health, 94,* 640–645.

Ervin, R. A., Gimpel Peacock, G., & Merrell, K. W. (2010). The school psychologist as a problem solver in the 21st century: Rational and role definition. In G. Gimpel Peacock, R. A. Ervin, D. J. Daly, & K. W. Merrell (Eds.), *Practical handbook of school psychology: Effective practices for the 21st century* (pp. 3–12). New York: Guilford Press.

Evans, J. (2000). Interventions to reduce repetition of deliberate self-harm. *International Review of Psychiatry, 12,* 44–47.

Farber, S. K. (2000). *When the body is the target: Self-harm, pain, and traumatic attachments.* Northvale, NJ: Jason Aronson.

Farberow, N. L. (Ed.). (1980). *The many faces of suicide: Indirect self-destructive behavior.* New York: McGraw-Hill.

Favaro, A., Ferrara, S., & Santonastoso, P. (2004). Impulsive and compulsive self-injurious behavior and eating disorders: An epidemiological study. In J. L. Levitt, R. A. Sansone, & L. Cohn (Eds.), *Self-harm behavior and eating disorders: Dynamics, assessment, and treatment* (pp. 31–43). New York: Brunner-Routledge.

Favazza, A. (1987). *Bodies under siege.* Baltimore, MD: Johns Hopkins University Press.

Favazza, A. (1996). *Bodies under siege: Self-mutilation and body modification in culture and psychiatry* (2nd ed.). Baltimore, MD: Johns Hopkins University Press.

Favazza, A. (1998). The coming of age of self-mutilation. *The Journal of Nervous and Mental Disease, 186,* 259–268.

Favazza, A., & Rosenthal, R. (1990). Varieties of pathological self-mutilation. *Behavioral Neurology, 3,* 77–85.

Fergusson, D. M., & Horwood, J. (1995). Predictive validity of categorically and dimensionally scored measures of disruptive childhood behaviors. *Journal of Clinical Child and Adolescent Psychology, 32,* 396–407.

Firestone, R. W., & Seiden, R. H. (1990). Suicide and the continuum of self-destructive behavior. *Journal of American College Health, 38,* 207–213.

FirstSigns. (2008a). LifeSIGNS self-injury factsheet for parents and guardians. http://www. firstsigns.org.uk/publications/. Retrieved 7 September 2008.

FirstSigns. (2008b). LifeSIGNS self-injury factsheet for teachers and lecturers. http://www. firstsigns.org.uk/publications/. Retrieved 7 September 2008.

FirstSigns. (2008c). LifeSIGNS self-injury factsheet for friends. http://www.firstsigns. org.uk/publications/. Retrieved 7 September 2008.

Fogt, J. B., Miller, D. N., & Zirkel, P. A. (2003). Defining autism: Professional best practices and published case law. *Journal of School Psychology, 41,* 201–216.

Fonagy, P., Gergely, G., Jurist, E., & Target, M. (2002). *Affect regulation, mentalization, and the development of self.* New York: Other Press.

Fredrickson, B. L., & Joiner, T. (2002). Positive emotions trigger upward spirals toward emotional well-being. *Psychological Science, 13,* 172–175.

Friedberg, R. D., & McClure, J. M. (2002). *Clinical practice of cognitive therapy with children and adolescents: The nuts and bolts.* New York: Guilford Press.

Froeschle, J., & Moyer, M. (2004). Just cut it out: Legal and ethical challenges in counseling students who self-mutilate. *Professional School Counseling, 7,* 231–236.

Furlong, M. J., O'Brennan, L., & Johnson, K. M. (2010). Test review of the BASC-2 Behavioral and Emotional Screening System. In K. F. Geisinger, R. A. Spies, & J. F. Carlson (Eds.), *The eighteenth mental measurements yearbook* [Electronic version]. http://www.unl.edu/buros. Retrieved 14 October 2009.

Gansle, K. A., & Noell, G. H. (2010). Assessment of skills in written expression within a problem-solving model. In G. Gimpel Peacock, R. A. Ervin, E. J. Daly, & K. W. Merrell (Eds.), *Practical handbook of school psychology: Effective practices for the 21st century* (pp. 99–114). New York: Guilford Press.

Garb, H. N. (1996). Taxometrics and the revision of diagnostic criteria. *American Psychologist, 51*, 553–554.

Garland, E. J. (2004). Facing the evidence: Antidepressant medication in children and adolescents. *Canadian Medical Association Journal, 170*, 489–491.

Gibbons, R. D., Brown, C. H., Hur, K., Marcus, A. M., Bhaumik, D. K., Erkens, J. A., et al. (2007). Early evidence on the effects of regulators' suicidality warnings on SSRI prescriptions and suicide in children and adolescents. *American Journal of Psychiatry, 164*, 1356–1363.

Gilman, R., Huebner, E. S., & Furlong, M. J. (Eds.). (2009). *Handbook of positive psychology in schools*. New York: Routledge.

Gimpel Peacock, G., Ervin, R. A., Daly, E. J., & Merrell, K. W. (Eds.). (2010). *Practical handbook of school psychology: Effective practices for the 21st century*. New York: Guilford Press.

Gittelman-Klein, R. (1986). Questioning the clinical usefulness of projective psychological tests for children. *Developmental and Behavioral Pediatrics, 7*, 378–382.

Glassman, L. H., Weierich, M. R., Hooley, J. M., Deliberto, T. L., & Nock, M. K. (2007). Child maltreatment, non-suicidal self-injury, and the mediating role of self-criticism. *Behaviour Research and Therapy, 45*, 2483–2490.

Goin, M. (2003). The "suicide prevention contract:" Dangerous myth. *Psychiatric News, 18*, 3.

Goodman, T. A. (2005). Working with children: Beginner's mind. In C. K. Germer, R. D. Siegel, & P. R. Fulton (Eds.), *Mindfulness and psychotherapy* (pp. 197–219). New York: Guilford Press.

Gordon, R. S. (1983). An operational classification of disease prevention. *U.S. Department of Health and Human Services Public Health Report 1983, 98*, 107–109.

Gratz, K. L. (2001). Measurement of deliberate self-harm: Preliminary data on the deliberate self-harm inventory. *Journal of Psychopathology and Behavioral Assessment, 23*, 253–263.

Gratz, K. L. (2003). Risk factors for and functions of deliberate self-harm: An empirical and conceptual review. *Clinical Psychology: Science and Practice, 10*, 192–205.

Gratz, K. L. (2006). Risk factors for deliberate self-harm among female college students: The role and interaction of childhood maltreatment, emotional inexpressivity, and affect intensity/reactivity. *American Journal of Orthopsychiatry, 76*, 238–250.

Gratz, K. L, & Roemer, L. (2004). Multidimensional assessment of emotion regulation and dys-regulation: Development, factor structure, and initial validation of the difficulties in emotion regulation scale. *Journal of Psychopathology and Behavioral Assessment, 26*, 41–54.

Greco, L. A., & Hayes, S. C. (Eds.). (2008). *Acceptance and mindfulness treatments for children and adolescents: A practitioner's guide*. Oakland, CA: New Harbinger Press.

Gresham, F. M. (2009). Foreword. In M. W. Steege & T. S. Watson, *Conducting school-based functional behavior assessments: A practitioner's guide* (2nd ed., pp. vii–viii). New York: Guilford Press.

Gresham, F. M., Watson, T. S., & Skinner, C. (2001). Functional behavioral assessment: Principles, procedures, and future directions. *School Psychology Review, 30*, 156.

Grossman, R., & Siever, L. (2001). Impulsive self-injurious behaviors: Neurobiology and psychopharmacology. In D. Simeon & E. Hollander (Eds.), *Self-injurious behaviors: Assessment and treatment* (pp. 117–148). Washington, DC: American Psychiatric Publishing.

Gureasko-Moore, D. P., DuPaul, G. J., & Power, T. J. (2005). Stimulant medication for attention-deficit/hyperactivity disorder: Medication monitoring practices of school psychologists. *School Psychology Review, 34*, 232–245.

Gutierrez, P. M., Osman, A., Barrios, F. X., & Kopper, B. A. (2001). Development and initial validation of the self-harm behavior questionnaire. *Journal of Personality Assessment, 77*, 475–490.

Gutierrez, P. M., Osman, A., & Kopper, B. A. (2000). Suicide risk assessment in a college student population. *Journal of Counseling Psychology, 47*, 403–413.

Gutkin, T. B. (2009). Ecological school psychology: A personal opinion and a plea for change. In T. B. Gutkin & C. R. Reynolds (Eds.), *The handbook of school psychology* (4th ed., pp. 463–496). New York: Wiley.

Haavisto, A., Sourander, A., Multimaki, P., Parkkola, K., Santalahti, P., Helenius, H., et al. (2005). Factors associated with ideation and acts of deliberate self-harm among 18-year-old boys: A prospective 10-year follow up study. *Social Psychiatry and Psychiatric Epidemiology, 40,* 912–921.

Haines, J., Williams, C. L., Brain, K. L., & Wilson, G. V. (1995). The psychophysiology of self-mutilation. *Journal of Abnormal Psychology, 104,* 471–489.

Hammad, T. A., Laughren, T., & Racoosin, J. (2006). Suicidality in pediatric patients treated with antidepressant drugs. *Archives of General Psychology, 63,* 332–339.

Hartman, D. (1996). Cutting among young people in adolescent units. *Therapeutic Communities, 17,* 5–17.

Harwood, H. (2000). *Updating estimates of the economic costs of alcohol abuse in the United States: Estimates, update methods, and data.* Report prepared by the Lewin Group for the National Institute on Alcohol Abuse and Alcoholism. Rockville, MD: National Institute of Mental Health.

Hawton, K., Fagg, J., Simkin, S., Bale, E., & Bond, A. (2000). Deliberate self-harm in adolescents in Oxford, 1985–1995. *Journal of Adolescence, 23,* 47–55.

Hawton, K., Sutton, L., Haw, C., Sinclair, J., & Harriss, L. (2005). Suicide and attempted suicide in bipolar disorder: a systemic review of risk factors. *Journal of Clinical Psychiatry, 66,* 693–704.

Hayes, S. C., Follette, V. M., & Linehan, M. M. (Eds.). (2004). *Mindfulness and acceptance: Expanding the cognitive-behavioral tradition.* New York: Guilford Press.

Hayes, S. C., & Greco, L. A. (2008). Acceptance and mindfulness for youth: It's time. In L. A. Greco & S. C Hayes (Eds.), *Acceptance and mindfulness treatments for children and adolescents: A practitioner's guide* (pp. 3–13). Oakland, CA: New Harbinger.

Hayes, S. C., Strosahl, K. D., & Wilson, K. G. (1999). *Acceptance and commitment therapy: An experiential approach to behavior change.* New York: Guilford Press.

Heath, N. L., & Nixon, M. K. (2009). Assessment of nonsuicidal self-injury in youth. In M. K. Nixon & N. L. Heath (Eds.), *Self-injury in youth: The essential guide to assessment and intervention.* New York: Routledge.

Heath, N. L., Schaub, K., Holly, S., & Nixon, M. K. (2009). Self-injury today: Review of population and clinical studies in adolescents. In M. K. Nixon & N. L. Heath (Eds.), *Self-injury in youth: The essential guide to assessment and intervention* (pp. 9–27). New York: Routledge.

Heath, N. L., Toste, J. R., & Beetham, E. (2006). "I am not well-equipped": High school teachers' perceptions of self-injury. *Canadian Journal of School Psychology, 21,* 73–92.

Hendin, H., Brent, D. A., Cornelius, J. R., Coyne-Beasley, T., Greenberg, T., Gould, M., et al. (2005). Youth suicide. In D. L. Evans, E. B. Foa, R. E. Gur, H. Hendline, C. P. O'Brien, M. E. P. Seligman, & B. T. Walsh (Eds.), *Treating and preventing adolescent mental health disorders* (pp. 434–493). New York: Oxford University Press.

Herpertz, S., Sass, H., & Favazza, A. (1997). Impulsivity in self-mutilative behavior: Psychometric and biological findings. *Journal of Psychiatric Research, 31,* 451–465.

Hilt, L. M., Cha, C. B., & Nolen-Hoeksema, S. (2008). Nonsuicidal self-injury in young adolescent girls: Moderators of the distress-function relationship. *Journal of Consulting and Clinical Psychology, 76,* 63–71.

Hilt, L. M., Nock, M. K., Lloyd-Richardson, E. E., & Prinstein, M. J. (2008). Longitudinal study of nonsuicidal self-injury among young adolescents: Rates, correlates, and preliminary test of an interpersonal model. *The Journal of Early Adolescence, 28,* 455–469.

Hojnoski, R. L., Morrison, R., Brown, M., & Matthews, W. J. (2006). Projective test use among school psychologists: A survey and critique. *Journal of Psychoeducational Assessment, 24,* 145–159.

Hollander, M. (2008). *Helping teens who cut: Understanding and ending self-injury.* New York: Guilford Press.

Horner, R. H., Sugai, G., Todd, A. W., & Lewis-Palmer, T. (2005). School-wide positive behavior support. In L. Bambara & L. Kern (Eds.), *Individualized supports for students with problem behaviors: Designing positive behavior support plans* (pp. 359–390). New York: Guilford Press.

Hosp, J. L., & Reschly, D. (2002). Regional differences in school psychology practice. *School Psychology Review, 31*, 11–29.

House, A. E. (1999, 2002). *DSM-IV diagnosis in the schools.* New York: Guilford Press.

Hughes, J. N., & Baker, D. B. (1991). *The clinical child interview.* New York: Guilford Press.

Hughes, T. L., Crothers, L. M., & Jimerson, S. R. (2008). *Identifying, assessing, and treating conduct disorder at school.* New York: Springer.

Individuals with Disabilities Education Improvement Act of 2004, 20 USC 1400.

Iwata, B. A., Pace, G. M., Dorsey, M. F., Zarcone, J. R., Vollmer, T. R., Smith, R. G., et al. (1994). The functions of self-injurious behavior: An experimental-epidemiological analysis. *Journal of Applied Behavior Analysis, 27*, 215–240.

Izutsu, T., Shimotsu, S., Matsumoto, T., Okada, T., Kikuchi, A., Kojimoto, M., et al. (2006). Deliberate self-harm and childhood hyperactivity in junior high school students. *European Child and Adolescent Psychiatry, 14*, 1–5.

Jablensky, A. (1999). The nature of psychiatric classification: Issues beyond ICD-10 and DSM-IV. *Australian and New Zealand Journal of Psychiatry, 33*, 137–144.

Jacob, S. (2009). Putting it all together: Implications for school psychology. *School Psychology Review, 38*, 239–243.

Jacob, S., & Hartshorne, T. S. (2007). *Ethics and law for school psychologists* (5th ed.). Hoboken, NJ: Wiley.

Jacobson, C. M., & Gould, M. (2007). The epidemiology and phenomenology of non-suicidal self-injurious behavior among adolescents: A critical review of the literature. *Archives of Suicide Research, 11*, 129–147.

Janis, I. B., & Nock, M. K. (2008). Behavioral forecasts do not improve the prediction of future behavior: A prospective study of self-injury. *Journal of Clinical Psychology, 64*, 1164–1174.

Jobes, D. A. (2003). *Manual for the collaborative assessment and management of suicidality – revised (CAMS-R).* Unpublished manuscript.

Johnson, K. M. (2010). Test review of the BASC-2 behavioral and emotional screening system. In K. F. Geisinger, R. A. Spies, & J. F. Carlson (Eds.), *The eighteenth mental measurements yearbook* [Electronic version].http://www.unl.edu/buros. Retrieved 14 October 2009.

Johnson, T. W., Brett, M. A., Roberts, L. F., & Wassersug, R. J. (2007). Eunuchs in contemporary society: Characterizing men who are voluntarily castrated (Part 1). *Journal of Sexual Medicine, 4*, 930–945.

Joiner, T. (2005). *Why people die by suicide.* Cambridge, MA: Harvard University Press.

Joiner, T. (2009). Suicide prevention in schools as viewed through the interpersonal-psychological theory of suicidal behavior. *School Psychology Review, 38*, 244–248.

Joiner, T. E., Van Orden, K. A., Witte, T. K., & Rudd, M. D. (2009). *The interpersonal theory of suicide: Guidance for working with suicidal clients.* Washington, DC: American Psychological Association.

Jones, K. M., & Wickstrom, K. F. (2010). Using functional assessment to select behavioral interventions. In G. Gimpel Peacock, R. A. Ervin, E. J. Daly, & K. W. Merrell (Eds.), *Practical handbook of school psychology: Effective practices for the 21st century* (pp. 192–210). New York: Guilford Press.

Kabat-Zinn, J. (1990). *Full catastrophe living: Using the wisdom of your body and mind to face stress, pain, and illness.* New York: Delacorte.

Kabat-Zinn, J. (1994). *Wherever you go, there you are: Mindfulness meditation in everyday life.* New York: Hyperion.

Kabat-Zinn, J. (2003). Mindfulness-based interventions in context: Past, present, and future. *Clinical Psychology: Science and Practice, 10*, 144–156.

Kamphaus, R. W., & Frick, J. P. (1996). *Clinical assessment of child and adolescent personality and behavior.* Needham Heights, MA: Allyn & Bacon.

Kamphaus, R. W., & Reynolds, C. R. (2007). *BASC-2 behavioral and emotional screening system.* Bloomington, MN: Pearson.

Kanan, L. M., Finger, J., & Plog, A. E. (2008). Self-injury and youth: Best practices for school intervention. *School Psychology Forum, 2*(2), 67–79.

Kavale, K. A., & Forness, S. R. (1999). Effectiveness of special education. In C. R. Reynolds & T. B. Gutkin (Eds.), *The handbook of school psychology* (pp. 984–1024). New York: Wiley.

Kearney, C. A. (2001). *School refusal behavior in youth: A functional approach to assessment and treatment.* Washington, DC: American Psychological Association.

Kearney, C. A. (2003). Bridging the gap among professionals who address youth with school absenteeism: Overview and suggestions for consensus. *Professional Psychology: Research and Practice, 34*, 57–65.

Kearney, C. A., Eisen, A. R., & Silverman, W. K. (1995). The legend and myth of school phobia. *School Psychology Quarterly, 10*, 65–85.

Kennedy, M. L., Faust, D., Willis, W. G., & Piotrowski, C. (1994). Social-emotional assessment practices in school psychology. *Journal of Psychoeducational Assessment, 12*, 228–240.

Kernberg, P. F. (1994). Psychological interventions for the suicidal adolescent. *American Journal of Psychotherapy, 48*, 52–63.

Kerr, M. M., & Nelson, C. M. (2002). *Strategies for addressing behavior problems in the classroom* (4th ed.). Upper Saddle River, NJ: Merrill Prentice-Hall.

Kettlewell, C. K. (1999). *Skin game.* New York: St. Martin's Griffin.

Klonsky, E. D. (2007). The functions of deliberate self-injury: A review of the evidence. *Clinical Psychology Review, 27*, 226–239.

Klonsky, E. D., & Glenn, C. R. (2009). Psychosocial risk and protective factors. In M. I. Nixon & N. L. Heath (Eds.), *Self-injury in youth: The essential guide to assessment and intervention* (pp. 45–58). New York: Routledge.

Klonsky, E. D., & Moyer, A. (2008). Childhood sexual abuse and non-suicidal self-injury: A meta-analysis. *British Journal of Psychiatry, 192*, 166–170.

Klonsky, E. D., & Muehlenkamp, J. J. (2007). Self injury: A research review for the practitioner. *Journal of Clinical Psychology: In Session, 63*, 1045–1056.

Klonsky, E. D., Oltmanns, T. F., & Turkheimer, E. (2003). Deliberate self-harm in a nonclinical population: Prevalence and psychological correlates. *American Journal of Psychiatry, 160*, 1501–1508.

Knoff, H. M. (2003). Evaluation of projective drawings. In C. R. Reynolds & R. W. Kamphaus (Eds.), *Handbook of psychological and educational assessment of children: Personality, behavior, and context* (pp. 91–158). New York: Guilford Press.

Kohlenberg, R. J., & Tsai, M. (1991). *Functional analytic psychotherapy: Creating intense and curative therapeutic relationships.* New York: Plenum Press.

Kratochvil, C. J., Vitiello, B., Walkup, J., Emslie, G., Waslick, B., Weller, E. B. et al. (2006). Selective serotonin reuptake inhibitors in pediatric depression: Is the balance between the benefits and risks favorable? *Journal of Child and Adolescent Psychopharmacology, 16*, 11–24.

Laraway, S., Snycerski, S., Michael, J., & Poling, A. (2003). Motivating operations and terms to describe them: Some further refinements. *Journal of Applied Behavior Analysis, 36*, 407–414.

Laye-Gindhu, A., & Schonert-Reichl, K. A. (2005). Non-suicidal self-harm among community adolescents: Understanding the "whats" and "whys" of self-harm. *Journal of Youth and Adolescence, 34*, 447–456.

Lesch, M., & Nyhan, W. I. (1964). A familial disorder or uric acid metabolism and central nervous system function. *American Journal of Medicine, 36*, 561–570.

Levenkron, S. (1998). *Cutting: Understanding and overcoming self-mutilation.* New York: Norton.

Levitt, S. (2004). *Self-harm behavior and eating disorders: Dynamics, assessment, and treatment.* Oxford: Routledge.

Levitt, V. H., & Merrell, K. W. (2009). Linking assessment to intervention for internalizing problems of children and adolescents. *School Psychology Forum, 3*(1), 13–26.

Levy, K. N., Yeomans, F. E., & Diamond, D. (2007). Psychodynamic treatments of self-injury. *Journal of Clinical Psychology: In Session*, 63, 1105–1120.

Libby, A. M., Brent, D. A., Morrato, E. J., Orton, H. D., Allen, R., & Valuck, R. J. (2007). Decline in treatment of pediatric depression after FDA advisory on risk of suicidality with SSRIs. *American Journal of Psychiatry, 164*, 884–891.

Lieberman, R. (2004). Understanding and responding to students who self-mutilate. *National Association of Secondary School Principals: Principal Leadership, 4*(7), 10–13.

Lieberman, R., & Poland, S. (2006). Self-mutilation. In G. G. Bear & K. M. Minke (Eds.), *Children's needs III: Development, prevention, and intervention* (pp. 965–976). Bethesda, MD: National Association of School Psychologists.

Lieberman, R. A., Toste, J. R., & Heath, N. L. (2009). Non-suicidal self-injury in the schools: Prevention and intervention. In M. K. Nixon & N. L. Heath (Eds.), *Self-injury in youth: The essential guide to assessment and intervention* (pp. 195–215). New York: Routledge.

Lightfoot, C. (1997). *The culture of adolescent risk-taking*. New York: Guilford Press.

Lilienfield, S. O., Wood, J. M., & Garb, H. N. (2000). The scientific status of projective techniques. *Psychological Science in the Public Interest, 1*, 27–65.

Linehan, M. M. (1993). *Cognitive-behavioral treatment of borderline personality disorder*. New York: Guilford Press.

Linehan, M. M. (2000). Behavioral treatments of suicidal behaviors: Definitional obfuscation and treatment outcomes. In R. W. Maris, S. S. Cannetto, J. L. McIntosh, & M. M. Silverman (Eds.), *Review of suicidology* (pp. 84–111). New York: Guilford Press.

Linehan, M. M., Comtois, K. A., Brown, M. Z., Heard, H. L., & Wagner, A. (2006). Suicide attempt self-injury interview (SASII): Development, reliability, and validity of a scale to assess suicide attempts and intentional self-injury. *Psychological Assessment, 18*, 303–312.

Little, S. G., & Rodemaker, J. E. (1998). Lesch-Nyhan disease. In L. Phelps (Ed.), *Health-related disorders in children and adolescents* (pp. 386–391). Washington, DC: American Psychological Association.

Lloyd, E. E., Kelley, M. L., & Hope, T. (1997). *Self-mutilation in a community sample of adolescents: Descriptive characteristics and provisional prevalence rates*. Poster presented at the Annual Meeting of the Society for Behavioral Medicine, New Orleans, LA.

Lloyd-Richardson, E. E., Nock, M. K., & Prinstein, M. J. (2009). Functions of adolescent nonsuicidal self-injury. In M. K. Nixon & N. L. Heath (Eds.), *Self-injury in youth: The essential guide to assessment and intervention* (pp. 29–41). New York: Routledge.

Lloyd-Richardson, E. E., Perrine, N., Dierker, L., & Kelley, M. L. (2007). Characteristics and functions of non-suicidal self-injury in a community sample of adolescents. *Psychological Medicine, 37*, 1183–1192.

Lofthouse, N., Muehlenkamp, J. J., & Adler, R. (2009). Non-suicidal self-injury and co-occurrence. In M. K. Nixon & N. L. Heath (Eds.), *Self-injury in youth: The essential guide to assessment and intervention* (pp. 59–78). New York: Routledge.

Lopez, S. J., Rose, S., Robinson, C., Marques, S. C., & Pais-Ribeiro, J. (2009). Measuring and promoting hope in schoolchildren. In R. Gilman, E. S. Huebner, & M. J. Furlong (Eds.), *Handbook of positive psychology in schools* (pp. 37–50). New York: Routledge.

Marcotte, A. M., & Hintze, J. M. (2010). Assessment of academic skills in reading within a problem-solving model. In G. Gimpel Peacock, R. A. Ervin, E. J. Daly, & K. W. Merrell (Eds.), *Practical handbook of school psychology: Effective practices for the 21ˢᵗ century* (pp. 67–85). New York: Guilford Press.

Martens, B. K., & Ardoin, S. P. (2010). Assessing disruptive behavior within a problem-solving model. In G. Gimpel Peacock, R. A. Ervin, E. J. Daly, & K. W. Merrell (Eds.), *Practical handbook of school psychology: Effective practices for the 21ˢᵗ century* (pp. 157–174). New York: Guilford Press.

Martinez, R. S., & Nellis, L. M. (2008). Response to intervention: A school-wide approach for promoting academic wellness for all students. In B. Doll & J. A. Cummings (Eds.), *Transforming school mental health services* (pp. 143–164). Thousand Oaks, CA: Corwin Press.

Mash, E. J., & Hunsley, J. (2005). Evidence-based assessment of child and adolescent disorders: Issues and challenges. *Journal of Clinical Child and Adolescent Psychology, 34*, 362–379.

Mazar-Mosiewicz, A., Pierson, E. E., & McIntosh, D. E. (2009). Legal issues in school health services and school psychology: Guidelines for the administration of medicine. *Psychology in the Schools, 46*, 813–819.

Mazza, J. J., & Reynolds, W. M. (2008). School-wide approaches to prevention of and intervention for depression and suicidal behaviors. In B. Doll & J. A. Cummings (Eds.), *Transforming school mental health services* (pp. 213–241). Thousand Oaks, CA: Corwin Press.

McCabe, P. C., & Robinson, F. (2008). Committing to social justice: The behavioral intention of school psychology and education trainees to advocate for lesbian, gay, bisexual, and transgendered youth. *School Psychology Review, 37*, 469–486.

McConaughy, S. H. (2005). *Clinical interviews for children and adolescents: Assessment to intervention.* New York: Guilford Press.

McCormick, P. (2000). *Cut.* New York: Scholastic.

McDonald, C. (2006). Self-mutilation in adolescents. *Journal of School Nursing, 22*, 193–200.

McKenna, K. Y. A., & Bargh, J. A. (2000). Plan 9 from cyberspace: The implications of the Internet for personality and social psychology. *Personality and Social Psychology Review, 4*, 57–75.

McVey-Noble, M. E. (2006). *When your child is cutting: A parent's guide to helping children overcome self-injury.* Oakland, CA: New Harbinger.

Meehl, P. E. (1995). Bootstraps taxometrics: Solving the classification problems in psychopathology. *American Psychologist, 50*, 266–275.

Meichenbaum, D. (1977). *Cognitive behavior modification: An integrative approach.* New York: Plenum Press.

Menninger, K. (1966). *Man against himself.* New York: Harcourt, Brace Janovich. (Original work published 1938).

Merrell, K. W. (2008a). *Helping students overcome depression and anxiety: A practical guide* (2nd ed.). New York: Guilford Press.

Merrell, K. W. (2008b). *Behavioral, social, and emotional assessment of children and adolescents* (3rd ed.). Mahwah, NJ: Lawrence Erlbaum.

Merrell, K. W., Ervin, R. A., & Gimpel, G. A. (2006). *School psychology for the 21st century: Foundations and practices.* New York: Guilford Press.

Merrell, K. W., Gueldner, B. A., & Tran, O. K. (2008). Social and emotional learning: A school-wide approach to intervention for socialization, friendship problems, and more. In B. Doll & J. A. Cummings (Eds.), *Transforming school mental health services* (pp. 165–185). Thousand Oaks, CA: Corwin Press.

Messer, J. M., & Fremouw, W. J. (2008). A critical review of explanatory models for self-mutilating behaviors in adolescents. *Clinical Psychology Review, 28*, 162–178.

Miller, D. N. (2010). Assessing internalizing problems and well-being. In G. Gimpel-Peacock, R. Ervin, E. Daly, & K. W. Merrell (Eds.), *Practical handbook of school psychology* (pp. 175–191). New York: Guilford Press.

Miller, D. N. (in press). *Child and adolescent suicidal behavior: School-based prevention, assessment, and intervention.* New York: Guilford Press.

Miller, F., & Bashkin, E. A. (1974). Depersonalization and self-mutilation. *Psychoanalytic Quarterly, 43*, 638–649.

Miller, D. N., & Eckert, T. L. (2009). Youth suicidal behavior: An introduction and overview. *School Psychology Review, 38*, 153–167.

Miller, D. N., Eckert, T. L., & Mazza, J. J. (2009). Suicide prevention programs in the schools: A review and public health perspective. *School Psychology Review, 38*, 168–188.

Miller, D. N., Gilman, R., & Martens, M. P. (2008). Wellness promotion in the schools: Enhancing students' mental and physical health. *Psychology in the Schools, 45*, 5–15.

Miller, D. N., & Jome, L. M. (2008). School psychologists and the assessment of childhood internalizing disorders: Perceived knowledge, role preferences, and training needs. *School Psychology International, 29*, 500–510.

Miller, D. N., & Jome, L. M. (in press). School psychologists and the secret illness: Perceived knowledge, role preferences, and training needs in the prevention and treatment of internalizing disorders. *School Psychology International.*

Miller, D. N., & McConaughy, S. H. (2005). Assessing risk for suicide. In S. H. McConaughy (Ed.), *Clinical interviews for children and adolescents: Assessment to intervention* (pp. 184–199). New York: Guilford Press.

Miller, D. N., & Nickerson, A. B. (2006). Projective assessment and school psychology: Contemporary validity issues and implications for practice. *The California School Psychologist, 11*, 73–84.

Miller, D. N., & Nickerson, A. B. (2007a). Projective techniques and the school-based assessment of childhood internalizing disorders: A critical analysis. *Journal of Projective Psychology and Mental Health, 14*, 48–58.

Miller, D. N., & Nickerson, A. B. (2007b). Changing the past, present, and future: Potential applications of positive psychology in school-based psychotherapy with children and youth. *Journal of Applied School Psychology, 24*, 147–162.

Miller, D. N., Nickerson, A. B., & Jimerson, S. R. (2009). Positive psychology and school-based interventions. In R. Gilman, E. S. Huebner, & M. Furlong (Eds.), *Handbook of positive psychology in schools* (pp. 293–304). New York: Routledge.

Miller, A. L., Rathus, J. H., & Linehan, M. M. (2007). *Dialectical behavior therapy with suicidal adolescents.* New York: Guilford Press.

Miller, D. N., & Sawka-Miller, K. D. (2008). The practice of school psychology in the 21st century: Reflections and recommendations. In D. Molina (Ed.), *School psychology 21ˢᵗ century issues and challenges* (pp. 1–11). New York: Nova Science.

Miller, D. N., & Sawka-Miller, K. D. (2009). A school-based preferential option for the poor: Child poverty, social justice, and a public health approach to intervention. In F. Columbus (Ed.), *Low incomes: Social, health, and educational impacts* (pp. 31–56). New York: Nova.

Motta, R. W., Little, S. G., & Tobin, M. I. (1993). The use and abuse of human figure drawings. *School Psychology Quarterly, 8*, 162–169.

Muehlenkamp, J. J. (2005). Self-injurious behavior as a separate clinical syndrome. *American Journal of Orthopsychiatry, 75*, 324–333.

Muehlenkamp, J. J. (2006). Empirically supported treatments and general therapy guidelines for non-suicidal self-injury. *Journal of Mental Health Counseling, 28*, 166–185.

Muehlenkamp, J. J., Engel, S. G., Wadeson, A., Crosby, R. D., Wonderlich, S. A., Simonich, H., & Mitchell, J. E. (2009). Emotional states preceding and following acts of non-suicidal self-injury in bulimia nervosa patients. *Behaviour Research and Therapy, 47*, 83–87.

Muehlenkamp, J. J., & Gutierrez, P. M. (2004). An investigation of differences between self-injurious behavior and suicide attempts in a sample of adolescents. *Suicide and Life-Threatening Behavior, 34*, 12–23.

Muehlenkamp, J. J., & Gutierrez, P. M. (2007). Risk for suicide attempts among adolescents who engage in non-suicidal self-injury. *Archives of Suicide Research, 11*, 69–82.

Muehlenkamp, J. J., Walsh, B. W., & McDade, M. (2010). Preventing non-suicidal self-injury in adolescents: The signs of self-injury program. *Journal of Youth and Adolescence, 39*, 306–314.

Nafisi, N., & Stanley, B. (2007). Developing and maintaining the therapeutic alliance with self-injuring patients. *Journal of Clinical Psychology: In Session, 63*, 1069–1079.

Naglieri, J. A. (1993). Human figure drawings in perspective. *School Psychology Quarterly, 8*, 170–176.

Nastasi, B. K. (2004). Meeting the challenges of the future: Integrating public health and public education for mental health promotion. *Journal of Educational and Psychological Consultation, 15*, 295–312.

Nastasi, B. K. (2008). Social justice and school psychology. *School Psychology Review, 37,* 487–492.

Nelson, C. M. (1992). Searching for meaning in the behavior of antisocial pupils, public school educators, and lawmakers. *School Psychology Review, 21,* 35–39.

Nickerson, A. B., Reeves, M. A., Brock, S. E., & Jimerson, S. R. (2009). *Identifying, assessing, and treating PTSD at school.* New York: Springer.

Nixon, M. K., Aulakh, H., Townsend, L., & Atherton, M. (2009). Psychological interventions for adolescents. In M. K. Nixon & N. L. Heath (Eds.), *Self-injury in youth: The essential guide to assessment and intervention* (pp. 217–236). New York: Routledge.

Nixon, M. K., Cloutier, P. F., & Aggarwal, S. (2002). Affect regulation and addictive aspects of repetitive self-injury in hospitalized adolescents. *Journal of the American Academy of Child & Adolescent Psychiatry, 41,* 1333–1341.

Nixon, M. K., & Heath, N. L. (2009a). Introduction to non-suicidal self-injury in adolescents. In M. K. Nixon & N. L. Heath (Eds.), *Self-injury in youth: The essential guide to assessment and intervention* (pp. 1–6). New York: Routledge.

Nixon, M. K., & Heath, N. L. (Eds.). (2009b). *Self-injury in youth: The essential guide to assessment and intervention.* New York: Routledge.

Nock, M. K. (Ed.). (2009). *Understanding nonsuicidal self-injury: Origins, assessment, and treatment.* Washington, DC: American Psychological Association.

Nock, M. K., Holmberg, E. B., Photos, V. I., & Michel, B. D. (2007). The self-injurious thoughts and behaviors interview: Development, reliability, and validity in an adolescent sample. *Psychological Assessment, 19,* 309–317.

Nock, M. K., Joiner, T. E., Gordon, K. H., Lloyd-Richardson, E., & Prinstein, M. J. (2006). Non-suicidal self-injury among adolescents: Diagnostic correlates and relation to suicide attempts. *Psychiatry Research, 144,* 65–72.

Nock, M. K., & Mendes, W. B. (2008). Physiological arousal, distress tolerance, and social problem-solving deficits among adolescent self-injurers. *Journal of Consulting and Clinical Psychology, 76,* 228–238.

Nock, M. K., & Prinstein, M. J. (2004). A functional approach to the assessment of self-mutilative behavior. *Journal of Consulting and Clinical Psychology, 72,* 885–890.

Nock, M. K., & Prinstein, M. J. (2005). Contextual features and behavioral functions of self-mutilation among adolescents. *Journal of Abnormal Psychology, 114,* 140–146.

Nock, M. K., Teper, R., & Hollander, M. (2007). Psychological treatment of self-injury among adolescents. *Journal of Clinical Psychology: In Session, 63,* 1081–1089.

Noggle, C. A., & Dean, R. S. (2009). Use and impact of antidepressants in the school setting. *Psychology in the Schools, 46,* 857–868.

Noll, J. G., Horowitz, L. A., Bonanno, G. A., Trickett, P. K., & Putnam, F. W. (2003). Revictimization and self-harm in females who experienced childhood sexual abuse. *Journal of Interpersonal Violence, 18,* 1452–1471.

Nose, M., Cipriani, A., & Biancosino, B. (2006). Efficacy of pharmacotherapy against core traits of borderline personality disorder: Meta-analysis of randomized controlled trials. *International Clinical Psychopharmacology, 21,* 345–353.

O'Brien, K. M., Larson, C. M., & Murrell, A. R. (2008). Third-wave behavior therapies for children and adolescents: Progress, challenges, and future directions. In L. A. Greco & S. C. Hayes (Eds.), *Acceptance and mindfulness treatments for children and adolescents: A practitioner's guide* (pp. 15–35). Oakland, CA: New Harbinger.

Osuch, E. A., Noll, G. G., & Putnam, F. W. (1999). The motivations for self-injury in psychiatric inpatients. *Psychiatry, 62,* 334–346.

Osuch, E. A., & Payne, G. W. (2009). Neurobiological perspectives on non-suicidal self-injury. In M. K. Nixon & N. L. Heath (Eds.), *Self-injury in youth: The essential guide to assessment and intervention* (pp. 79–110). London, UK: Routledge.

Paivio, S. C., & McCulloch, C. R. (2004). Alexithymia as a mediator between childhood trauma and self-injurious behaviors. *Child Abuse and Neglect, 28,* 339–354.

Pattison, E. M., & Kahan, J. (1983). The deliberate self-harm syndrome. *American Journal of Psychiatry, 140*, 867–872.

Peterson, C. (2006). *A primer in positive psychology.* New York: Oxford University Press.

Pierson, E. E. (2009a). Introduction to the special issue: Psychopharmacology and the practice of school psychology. *Psychology in the Schools, 46*, 805.

Pierson, E. E. (2009b). Antidepressants and suicidal ideation in adolescence: A paradoxical effect. *Psychology in the Schools, 46*, 910–914.

Pitcher, G., & Poland, S. (1992). *Crisis intervention in the schools.* New York: Guilford Press.

Plante, L. G. (2007). *Bleeding to ease the pain: Cutting, self-injury, and the adolescent search for self.* Westport, CT: Praeger.

Plener, P. L., Libal, G., & Nixon, M. K. (2009). Use of medication in the treatment of nonsuicidal self-injury in youth. In M. K. Nixon & N. L. Heath (Eds.), *Self-injury in youth: The essential guide to assessment and intervention* (pp. 275–308). New York: Routledge.

Plener, P. L., & Muehlenkamp, J. (2007). Correspondence: Letter to the editor. *Psychological Medicine, 37*, 1.

Poland, S. (1989). *Suicide intervention in the schools.* New York: Guilford Press.

Poland, S., & McCormick, J. (1999). *Coping with crisis: Lessons learned. A complete and comprehensive guide to school crisis intervention.* Longmont, CO: Sopris West.

Pollock, L. R., & Williams, J. M. G. (1998). Problem solving and suicidal behavior. *Suicide and Life-Threatening Behavior, 28*, 375–387.

Ponton, L. E. (1997). *The romance of risk: Why teenagers do the things they do.* New York: Basic Books.

Power, T. J. (2003). Promoting children's mental health: Reform through interdisciplinary and community partnerships. *School Psychology Review, 32*, 3–16.

Prasse, D. P. (2002). Best practices in school psychology and the law. In A. Thomas & J. Grimes (Eds.), *Best practices in school psychology IV* (pp. 3–20). Bethesda, MD: National Association of School Psychologists.

Ramsay, R. F., Tanney, B. L., Lang, W. A., & Kinzel, T. (2004). *Suicide intervention handbook* (10th ed.). Calgary, AB: LivingWorks.

Rehabilitation Act of 1973, Pub. L. No. 93-112, 87 Stat. 355 (codified as amended in scattered sections of 15 U.S.C., 20 U.S.C., 29 U.S.C., 36 U.S.C., 41 U.S.C., and 42 U.S.C.).

Reschly, D. J. (2008). School psychology paradigm shift and beyond. In A. Thomas & A. J. Grimes (Eds.), *Best practices in school psychology V* (Vol. 1, pp. 3–15). Bethesda, MD: National Association of School Psychologists.

Reynolds, C. R., & Kamphaus, R. W. (2004). *Behavior assessment system for children* (2nd ed.). Circle Pines, MN: AGS.

Reynolds, W. M. (1988). *Suicidal ideation questionnaire: Professional manual.* Odessa, FL: Psychological Assessment Resources.

Reynolds, W. M., & Mazza, J. J. (1993). *Suicidal behavior in adolescents: Suicide attempts in school-based youngsters.* Unpublished manuscript.

Riley-Tillman, T. C., & Burns, M. K. (2009). *Evaluating educational interventions: Single-case design for measuring response to intervention.* New York: Guilford Press.

Rodham, K., Hawton, K., & Evans, E. (2004). Reasons for deliberate self-harm: Comparison of self-poisoners and self-cutters in a community sample of adolescents. *Journal of the American Academy of Child and Adolescent Psychiatry, 43*, 80–87.

Rogers, M. R., & O'Bryon, E. C. (2008). Advocating for social justice: The context for change in school psychology. *School Psychology Review, 37*, 493–498.

Ross, W. D. (1930). *The right and the good.* Oxford: Clarendon Press.

Ross, S., & Heath, N. (2002). A study of the frequency of self-mutilation in a community sample of adolescents. *Journal of Youth and Adolescence, 31*, 67–77.

Ross, S., Heath, N. L., & Toste, J. R. (2009). Non-suicidal self-injury and eating pathology in high school students. *American Journal of Orthopsychiatry, 79*, 83–92.

Ross, R. R., & McKay, H. R. (1979). *Self-mutilation.* Lexington, MA: Lexington Books.

Rudd, M. D., Mandrusiak, M., & Joiner, T. E. (2006). The case against no-suicide contracts: The commitment to treatment statement as a practice alternative. *Journal of Clinical Psychology, 62,* 243–251.

Salvia, J., & Ysseldyke, J. E. (2001). *Assessment in special and remedial education* (8th ed.). Boston, MA: Houghton Mifflin.

Sandoval, J. (Ed.). (2002). *Handbook of crisis counseling, intervention, and prevention in the Schools* (2nd ed.). Hillsdale, NJ: Lawrence Erlbaum.

Sandoval, J., & Brock, S. E. (2009). Managing crisis: Prevention, intervention, and treatment. In T. B. Gutkin & C. R. Reynolds (Eds.), *The handbook of school psychology* (4th ed., pp. 886–904). New York: Wiley.

Sandoval, J., & Zadeh, S. (2008). Principles of intervening with suicide. *School Psychology Forum, 2*(2), 49–66.

Sansone, R. A., & Levitt, J. L. (2004). The prevalence of self-harm behavior in those with eating disorders. In J. L. Levitt, R. S. Sansone, & L. Cohn (Eds.), *Self-harm behavior and eating disorders: Dynamics, assessment, and treatment* (pp. 3–14). New York: Brunner-Routledge.

Sansone, R. A., Wiederman, M. W., & Sansone, L. A. (1998). The self-harm inventory (SHI): Development of a scale for identifying self-destructive behaviors and borderline personality disorder. *Journal of Clinical Psychology, 54,* 973–983.

Sawka, K. D., McCurdy, B. L., & Mannella, M. C. (2002). Strengthening emotional support services: An empirically based model for training teachers of students with behavior disorders. *Journal of Emotional and Behavioral Disorders, 10,* 223–232.

Schulte, A. C., Osborne, S. S., & Erchul, W. P. (1998). Effective special education: A United Stated dilemma. *School Psychology Review, 27,* 66–76.

Segal, Z. V., Williams, J. M. G., & Teasdale, J. D. (2002). *Mindfulness-based cognitive therapy for depression: A new approach to preventing relapse.* New York: Guilford Press.

Seligman, M. E. P. (1992). *Helplessness: On depression, development, and death.* New York: Freeman.

Shapiro, S. (2008). Addressing self-injury in the school setting. *The Journal of School Nursing, 24,* 124–130.

Shapiro, L. E. (2008). *Stopping the pain: A workbook for teens who cut and self-injure.* Oakland, CA: New Harbinger.

Shapiro, E. S., & Heick, P. F. (2004). School psychologist assessment practices in the evaluation of students referred for social/behavioral/emotional problems. *Psychology in the Schools, 41,* 551–561.

Shneidman, E. S. (1985). *Definition of suicide.* New York: Wiley.

Shneidman, E. S. (1996). *The suicidal mind.* New York: Oxford University Press.

Shriberg, D. (2009). Social justice and school mental health: Evolution and implications for practice. In J. M. Jones (Ed.), *The psychology of multiculturalism in the schools: A primer for practice, training, and research* (pp. 49–65). Bethesda, MD: National Association of School Psychologists.

Shriberg, D., Bonner, M., Sarr, B. J., Walker, A. M., Hyland, M., & Chester, C. (2008). Social justice through a school psychology lens: Definition and applications. *School Psychology Review, 37,* 453–468.

Simeon, D., & Favazza, A. (2001). Self-injurious behaviors: Phenomenology and assessment. In D. Simeon & E. Hollander (Eds.), *Self-injurious behaviors, assessment and treatment* (pp. 1–28). Washington, DC: American Psychiatric Publishing.

Simeon, D., & Hollander, E. (2001). (Eds.). *Self-injurious behaviors: Assessment and treatment.* Washington, DC: American Psychiatric Publishing.

Skiba, R., & Grizzle, K. (1991). The social maladjustment exclusion: Issues of definition and assessment. *School Psychology Review, 20,* 580–594.

Skinner, B. F. (1938). *The behavior of organisms: An experimental analysis.* New York: Appleton-Century.

Skinner, B. F. (1953). *Science and human behavior.* New York: Free Press.

Snyder, C. R., & Lopez, S. J. (2007). *Positive psychology: The scientific and practical exploration of human strengths.* Thousand Oaks, CA: Sage.

Sourander, A., Aromaa, A., Pihalkoski, L., Haavisto, A., Rautava, P., Helenius, H., et al. (2006). Early predictors of deliberate self-harm among adolescents: A prospective follow-up study from age 3 to age 15. *Journal of Affective Disorders, 93,* 87–96.

Speckens, A. E. M., & Hawton, K. (2005). Social problem solving in adolescents with suicidal behavior: A systematic review. *Suicide and Life-Threatening Behavior, 35,* 365–387.

Sroufe, L. A. (1997). Psychopathology as an outcome of development. *Development and Psychopathology, 9,* 251–268.

Stanley, B., Winchel, R., Molcho, A., Simeon, D., & Stanley, M. (1992). Suicide and the self-harm continuum: Phenomenological and biochemical evidence. *International Review of Psychiatry, 4,* 149–155.

Steege, M. W., & Watson, T. S. (2009). *Conducting school-based functional behavioral assessments: A practitioner's guide* (2nd ed.). New York: Guilford Press.

Strein, W., Hoagwood, K., & Cohn, A. (2003). School psychology: A public health perspective II. Prevention, populations, and systems change. *Journal of School Psychology, 41,* 23–38.

Strong, M. (1998). *A bright red scream: Self-mutilation and the language of pain.* New York: Penguin.

Sugai, G. (2007). Promoting behavioral competence in schools: A commentary on exemplary practices. *Psychology in the Schools, 44,* 113–118.

Suldo, S. M., Huebner, E. S., Friedrich, A. A., & Gilman, R. (2009). Life satisfaction. In R. Gilman, E. S. Huebner, & M. J. Furlong (Eds.), *Handbook of positive psychology in schools* (pp. 27–35). New York: Routledge.

Suyemoto, K. L. (1998). The functions of self-mutilation. *Clinical Psychology Review, 18,* 531–554.

Suyemoto, K. L., & MacDonald, M. L. (1995). Self-cutting in female adolescents. *Psychotherapy, 32,* 162–171.

Swearer, S. M., Espelage, D. L., Brey Love, K., & Kingsbury, W. (2008). School-wide approaches to intervention for school aggression and bullying. In B. Doll & J. Cummings (Eds.), *Transforming school mental health services* (pp. 187–212). Thousand Oaks, CA: Corwin Press.

Tilly, W. D. (2008). The evolution of school psychology to science-based practice: Problem solving and the three-tiered model. In A. Thomas & A. J. Grimes (Eds.), *Best practices in school psychology V* (Vol. 1, pp. 17–36). Bethesda, MD: National Association of School Psychologists.

Tolmunen, T., Rissanen, M. L., Hintikka, J., Maaranen, P., Honkalampi, K., Kylmä, J., & Laukkanen, E. (2008). Dissociation, self-cutting, and other self-harm behavior in a general population of Finnish adolescents. *Journal of Nervous and Mental Disease, 196,* 768–771.

Van der Kolk, B. A. (2005). Developmental trauma disorder: Toward a rational diagnosis for children with complex trauma histories. *Psychiatric Annals, 35,* 401–408.

Van der Kolk, B. A., McFarlane, A. C., & Wiesaeth, L. (Eds.). (1996). *Traumatic stress.* New York: Guilford Press.

Vega, V. (2007). *Comes the darkness, comes the light: A memoir of cutting, healing, and hope.* New York: AMACOM/American Management Association.

Volpe, R. J., Heick, P. F., & Gureasko-Moore, D. P. (2005). An agile behavioral model for monitoring the effects of stimulant medication in school settings. *Psychology in the Schools, 42,* 509–523.

Wagner, E. E., Rathus, J. H., & Miller, A. L. (2006). Mindfulness in dialectical behavior therapy (DBT) for adolescents. In R. A. Baer (Ed.), *Mindfulness-based treatment approaches: Clinician's guide to evidence base and applications* (pp. 167–189). San Diego, CA: Elsevier.

Walker, H. M., Horner, R. H., Sugai, G., Bullis, M., Sprague, J. R., Bricker, D., et al. (1996). Integrated approaches to preventing antisocial behavior patterns among school-age children and youth. *Journal of Emotional and Behavioral Disorders, 4,* 193–256.

Walsh, B. W. (2006). *Treating self-injury: A practical guide.* New York: Guilford Press.

Walsh, B. W. (2007). Clinical assessment of self-injury: A practical guide. *Journal of Clinical Psychology: In Session, 63*, 1057–1068.

Walsh, B. W., & Rosen, P. M. (1988). *Self-mutilation: Theory, research, & treatment.* New York: Guilford Press.

Weierich, M. R., & Nock, M. K. (2008). Posttraumatic stress symptoms mediate the relationship between childhood sexual abuse and nonsuicidal self-injury. *Journal of Consulting and Clinical Psychology, 76*, 39–44.

Whitlock, J., Eckenrode, J., & Silverman, D. (2006). Self-injurious behaviors in a college population. *Pediatrics, 117*, 1939–1948.

Whitlock, J., Lader, W., & Conterio, K. (2007). The Internet and self-injury: What psychotherapists should know. *Journal of Clinical Psychology: In Session, 63*, 1135–1143.

Whitlock, J. L., Eels, G., Cummings, N., & Purington, A. (2009). Non-suicidal self-injury on college campuses: Mental health provider assessment of prevalence and need. *Journal of College Student Psychotherapy, 23*, 172–183.

Whitlock, J. L., Powers, J. L., & Eckenrode, J. (2006). The virtual cutting edge: The Internet and adolescent self-injury. *Developmental Psychology, 42*, 407–417.

Wilber, T. (2007, September 24). Number of self-injuring youths on rise. *Binghamton Press and Sun-Bulletin*, pp. 1A, 6A.

Wilson, M. S., & Reschly, D. J. (1996). Assessment in school psychology training and practice. *School Psychology Review, 25*, 9–23.

Winchel, R. M., & Stanley, M. (1991). Self-injurious behavior: A review of the behavior and biology of self-mutilation. *American Journal of Psychiatry, 148*, 306–317.

Wingate, L. R., Burns, A. B., Gordon, K. H., Perez, M., Walker, R. L., Williams, F. M. et al. (2006). Suicide and positive cognitions: Positive psychology applied to the understanding and treatment of suicidal behavior. In T. E. Ellis (Ed.), *Cognition and suicide: Theory, research, and therapy* (pp. 261–283). Washington, DC: American Psychological Association.

Winkler, K. (2003). *Cutting and self-mutilation: When teens injure themselves.* Berkeley Heights, NJ: Enslow Publishers.

Wong, I. C., Besag, F. M., Santosh, P. J., & Murray, M. L. (2004). Use of selective serotonin reuptake inhibitors in children and adolescents. *Drug Safety, 27*, 991–1000.

Woodberry, K. A., Roy, R., & Indik, J. (2008). Dialectical behavior therapy for adolescents with borderline features. In L. A. Greco & S. C. Hayes (Eds.), *Acceptance and mindfulness treatments for children and adolescents: A practitioner's guide* (pp. 115–138). Oakland, CA: New Harbinger Press.

Yalof, J., Abraham, P., Domingos, B., & Socket, B. (2001). Re-examining the Rorschach test in school psychology practice. *The School Psychologist, 55*, 97, 100–102, 110–112.

Yates, T. M. (2004). The developmental psychopathology of self-injurious behavior: Compensatory regulation in posttraumatic adaptation. *Clinical Psychology Review, 24*, 35–74.

Ysseldyke, J., Burns, M., Dawson, M., Kelly, B., Morrison, D., Ortiz, S., et al. (2006). *School psychology: A blueprint for training and practice III.* Bethesda, MD: National Association of School Psychologists.

Zila, L. M., & Kiselica, M. S. (2001). Understanding and counseling self-mutilation in female adolescents and young adults. *Journal of Counseling and Development, 79*, 46–52.

Zlotnick, C., Shea, M. T., Recupero, P., Bidadi, K., Pearlstein, T., & Brown, P. (1997). Trauma, dissociation, implusivity, and self-mutilation among substance abuse patients. *American Journal of Orthopsychiatry, 67*, 650–654.

Zoroglu, S. S., Tuzun, U., Sar, V., Tutkun, H., Savas, H. A., Ozturk, M., et al. (2003). Suicide attempts and self-mutilation among Turkish high school students in relation with abuse, neglect and dissociation. *Psychiatry & Clinical Neurosciences, 57*, 119–126.

Subject Index